Texas Gun Pros

License to Carry a Handgun

Class Notes

Advanced Carry Notes

Texas Concealed Handgun Laws

Contents

Steps to Obtaining Your Concealed Handgun License

1. Attend the Texas Gun Pros CHL course and obtain a signed CHL-100 form from the instructor(s).

2. Apply online at https://txapps.texas.gov/txapp/txdps/chl/

3. Upon completion of the online application you will be provided with the link to schedule your fingerprints with Identogo. https://tx.ibtfingerprint.com/. Note having your fingerprints on file from another state agency does not matter. You MUST have separate fingerprints for CHL.

4. We will email you a PDF copy of your CHL-100 class completion form. After applying for the license, go to the http://dps.texas.gov website, select the Concealed Handgun License Division (note, this may change to something else after January 1, 2016 when the license becomes a License to Carry (LTC) instead of a CHL) and select the Contact Us link. You'll again need to select the CHL department from a dropdown and in another dropdown, select "CHL Supporting documents." Fill out the form and upload the PDF that we sent you. If you have a receipt from the fingerprint place you can upload it, also, and if you're a veteran and want the reduced rate, or you're on Active Duty, you can upload the supporting documents to get the reduced fee.

Eligibility

Texas Government Code Subsection 411.172

A person is eligible for a license to carry a concealed handgun if the person:

1. is a legal resident of this state for the six-month period preceding the date of application under this subchapter or if the person relocates to this state with the intent to establish residency in this state.
2. is at least 21 years of age;
3. has not been convicted of a felony;
4. is not charged with the commission of a Class A or Class B misdemeanor or equivalent offense, or of an offense of Disorderly Conduct or equivalent offense, or of a felony under an information or indictment;
5. is not a fugitive from justice for a felony or a Class A or Class B misdemeanor or equivalent offense;
6. is not a chemically dependent person; ("Chemically dependent person" means a person who frequently or repeatedly becomes intoxicated by excessive indulgence in alcohol or uses controlled substances or dangerous drugs so as to acquire a fixed habit and an involuntary tendency to become intoxicated or use those substances as often as the opportunity is presented.)
7. is not incapable of exercising sound judgment with respect to the proper use and storage of a handgun;

    For purposes of this Subsection a person is incapable of exercising sound judgment with respect to the proper use and storage of a handgun if the person:

    - Has been diagnosed by a licensed physician as suffering from a psychiatric disorder or condition that causes or is likely to cause substantial impairment in judgment, mood, perception, impulse control, or intellectual ability;
    - Suffers from a psychiatric disorder or condition that:
        - is in remission but is reasonably likely to redevelop at a future time; or
        - requires continuous medical treatment to avoid redevelopment;
    - Has been diagnosed by a licensed physician, determined by a review board or similar authority, or declared by a court to be incompetent to manage the person's own affairs; or x Has entered in a criminal proceeding a plea of not guilty by reason of insanity.

    The following constitutes evidence that a person has a psychiatric disorder or condition:

    - Involuntary psychiatric hospitalization;
    - Psychiatric hospitalization;
    - Inpatient or residential substance abuse treatment in the preceding five-year period;
    - Diagnosis in the preceding five-year period by a licensed physician that the person is dependent on alcohol, a controlled substance, or a similar substance; or

- Diagnosis at any time by a licensed physician that the person suffers or has suffered from a psychiatric disorder or condition consisting of or relating to:
  - schizophrenia or delusional disorder;
  - bipolar disorder;
  - chronic dementia, whether caused by illness, brain defect, or brain injury;
  - dissociative identity disorder;
  - intermittent explosive disorder; or
  - anti-social personality disorder.

A person who has previously been diagnosed as suffering from a psychiatric disorder or condition is not because of that disorder or condition incapable of exercising sound judgment with respect to the proper use and storage of a handgun if the person provides the department with a certificate from a licensed physician whose primary practice is in the field of psychiatry stating that the psychiatric disorder or condition is in remission and is not reasonably likely to develop at a future time.

8. has not, in the five years preceding the date of application, been convicted of a Class A or Class B misdemeanor or equivalent offense or of an offense under Section 42.01, Penal Code, or equivalent offense;
9. is fully qualified under applicable federal and state law to purchase a handgun;
10. has not been finally determined to be delinquent in making a child support payment administered or collected by the attorney general;
11. has not been finally determined to be delinquent in the payment of a tax or other money collected by the comptroller, the tax collector of a political subdivision of the state, or any agency or subdivision of the state;
12. is not currently restricted under a court protective order or subject to a restraining order affecting the spousal relationship, other than a restraining order solely affecting property interests;
13. has not, in the 10 years preceding the date of application, been adjudicated as having engaged in delinquent conduct violating a penal law of the grade of felony; and
14. has not made any material misrepresentation, or failed to disclose any material fact, in an application submitted for a Concealed Handgun License.

A person who is at least 18 years of age but not yet 21 years of age is eligible for a license to carry a concealed handgun if the person:

- is a member or veteran of the United States Armed Forces, including a member or veteran of the Reserves or National Guard;
- was discharged under honorable conditions, if discharged from the United States Armed Forces, Reserves, or National Guard; and
- meets the other eligibility requirements of Subsection (a) except for the minimum age required by federal law to purchase a handgun.

The issuance of a license to carry a concealed handgun to a person eligible under Subsection (g) does not affect the person's ability to purchase a handgun or ammunition under federal law.

Federal Requirements for Purchasing a Gun

The following list of prohibited persons are ineligible to own firearms under the Brady Handgun Violence Prevention Act:

- Those convicted of felonies and certain misdemeanors except where state law reinstates rights, or removes disability
- Fugitives from justice
- Unlawful users of certain depressant, narcotic, or stimulant drugs
- Those adjudicated as mental defectives or incompetents or those committed to any mental institution and currently containing a dangerous mental illness
- Non-US citizens, unless permanently immigrating into the U.S. or in possession of a hunting license legally issued in the U.S.
- Illegal Aliens
- Those who have renounced U.S. citizenship
- Minors defined as under the age of eighteen for long guns and handguns, with the exception of Vermont, eligible at age sixteen
- Persons convicted in any court of a misdemeanor crime of domestic violence
- Persons under indictment for a crime punishable by imprisonment for more than one year are ineligible to receive, transport, or ship any firearm or ammunition

Handgun Use and Safety

Basic Rules for Safe Gun Handling

- ALWAYS keep the gun pointed in a safe direction.
- ALWAYS keep your finger off the trigger until ready to shoot.
- ALWAYS keep the gun unloaded until ready to use.

Expanded Rules for Safe Gun Handling

- Treat every gun as if it were loaded.
- Keep your muzzle pointed in a safe direction.
- Be sure of your target and what is in front of it and behind it.
- Check your ammunition. Right caliber? Flaws or defects?
- Know how to operate your gun and make sure it is in good operating order.
- Keep your finger off the trigger until ready to shoot!!!!
- Never use alcohol or drugs before or during shooting.
- Store guns so they are not accessible to unauthorized persons.

Safety Equipment

- Hearing protection (ear plugs or over the ear protection)
- Eye protection (prescription glasses will work)
- Clothing to protect from flying brass

REMEMBER!
Treat EVERY Gun
as if it were
LOADED!

- Some Semi-Automatic Pistols have external, manual safeties, some do not

- Some have De-cockers, some do not

- Some have hammers, some have strikers (internal hammers)

- ALL have internal safeties to prevent against accidental firing – the trigger MUST BE PULLED for them to go off

A Safety is a Mechanical Device That Can Fail

REMEMBER! Keep Your Finger OFF the Trigger Until Ready to Shoot

Causes of Firearm Accidents

IGNORANCE (Lack of Knowledge)

- Ignorance of rules for Safe Gun Handling
- Ignorance of the proper and safe way to operate a pistol

CARELESSNESS (Poor or Improper Attitude)

- Failure to apply rules for safe gun handling
- Failure to properly observe the procedures for safe gun operation

Shooting is 80% Mental and 20% Ability

MENTAL DISCIPLINE

- Confidence in Yourself and Your Firearm
- Positive Thinking
- Ability to employ the Fundamentals of Shooting

FUNDAMENTALS OF SHOOTING

- Sight Alignment/Sight Picture
- Trigger Control
- Breathing
- Grip
- Stance
- Follow Through

Determining Your Dominate Eye

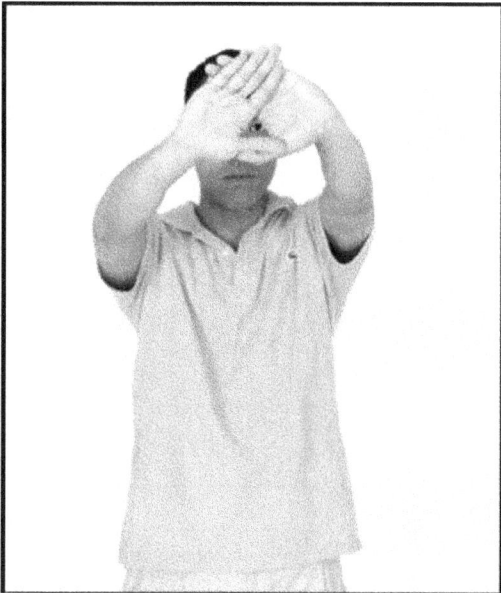

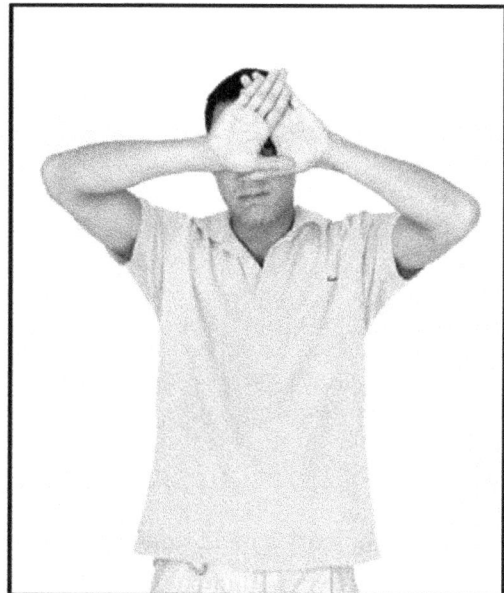

- Extend arms forward and form a small opening between your hands.
- Look at a distant object through the opening.
- Bring your hands to your face while looking at the object. The opening will be aligned with the dominant eye.

When aiming a handgun, align the firearm with your dominate eye. Both eyes should be open for maximum light.

Stance

- Comfortable, feet shoulder with apart
- Strong side foot, slightly back

Grip

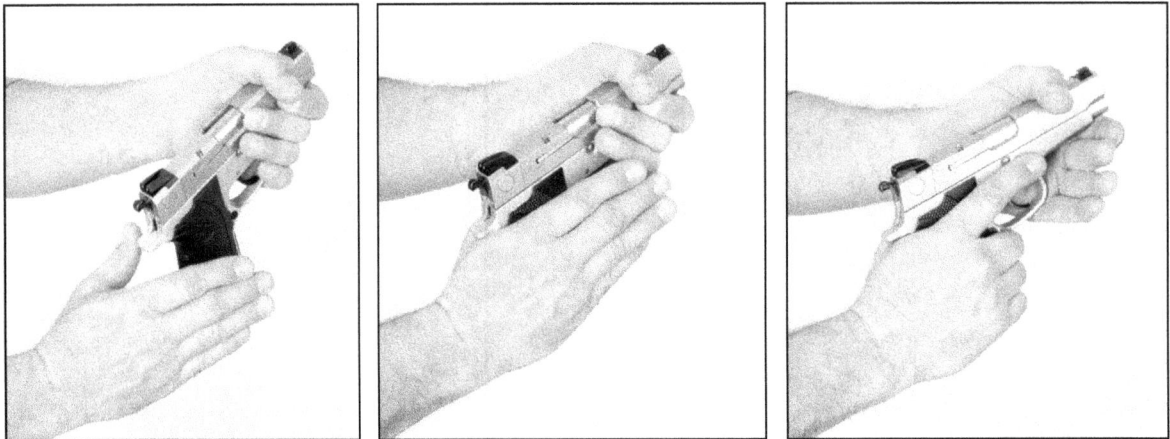

- Non-shooting hand safely puts pistol in shooting hand.
- "V" between thumb and forefinger of shooting hand is placed high on the pistol back strap.
- Pistol is gripped with the base of the thumb and lower three fingers. Grip pressure straight to the rear, trigger finger along frame.

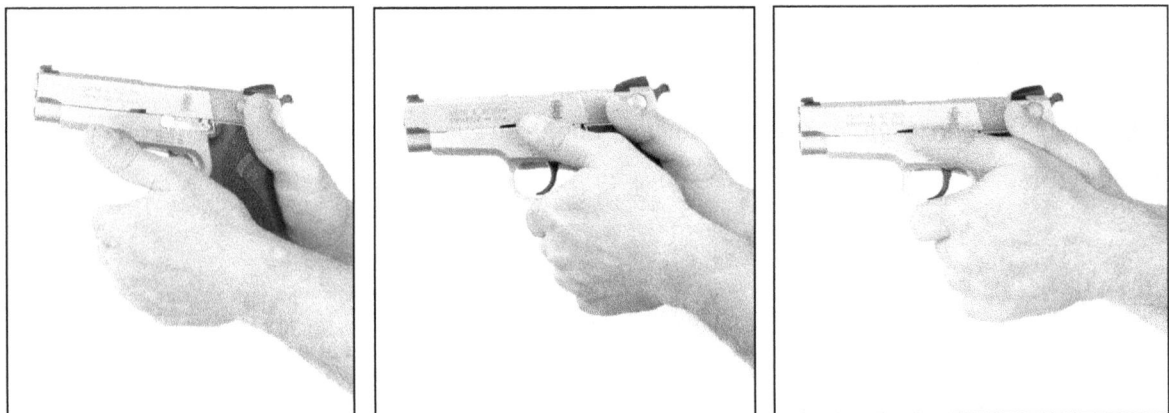

- Bring support hand to shooting hand.
- Wrap support-hand fingers around shooting-hand fingers.
- Bring heel of support hand firmly against heel of shooting hand.

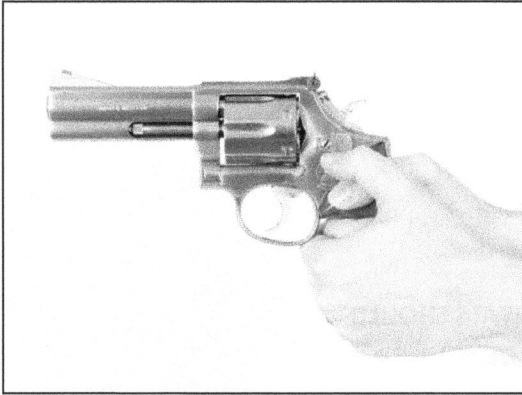

REVOLVER
Non-shooting hand thumb lies atop shooting hand thumb

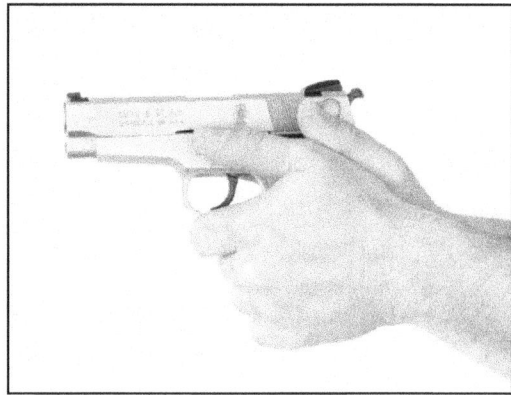

SEMI-AUTOMATIC
Non-shooting hand thumb is under shooting hand thumb

Crossing Thumbs = Getting Cut

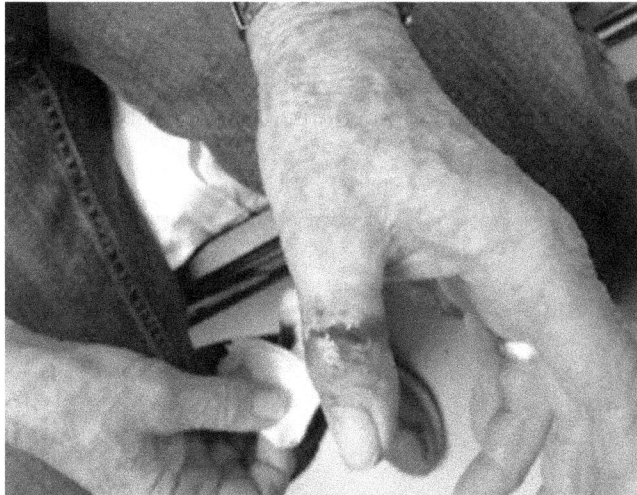

Keep thumbs on the same side

This was the result of crossing thumbs with a small gun.
It does not matter what size your semi-automatic gun is getting cut is a possibility.

Fundamentals of Pistol Shooting

- Aiming
- Hold Control
- Breath Control
- Trigger Control
- Follow-Through

**THESE FIVE FUNDAMENTALS SHOULD
BE PERFORMED WITH EVERY SHOT.**

Aiming

- AIMING is the process of achieving the proper relationship between the target, the front sight and the rear sight.
- AIMING consists of two components:
    - Sight Alignment
    - Sight Picture

Sight Alignment

- **SIGHT ALIGNMENT** refers to the proper relationship of the pistol's front and rear sights.
- With Post and Notch sights the top of the front and rear sights are even
- The front sight is centered in the rear notch.

Sight Picture

- Proper **SIGHT PICTURE** is obtained when the aligned sights are put into their proper relationship with the target.
- The front sight should be in focus when aiming.

Hold Control

- Hold Control allows the shooter to maintain proper sight alignment and sight picture while firing the shot.
- A proper grip is critical to Hold Control
- One goal of hold control is to minimize the arc of movement.

ARC OF MOVEMENT

Refers to the unavoidable motion of a pistol held in a shooting position. Practice decreases the arc of movement.

Breath Control

- BREATH CONTROL minimizes the body movement produced by breathing, which can impair good shooting.
- Take a breath before each shot, let out enough air to be comfortable, then simply stop breathing while firing the shot.
- Avoid holding the breath too long. This can cause tremors.

Trigger Control

- TRIGGER CONTROL is the proper method of activating the trigger to minimize movement that can misalign the sights.
- Utilize the pad of your index finger.
- Squeeze the trigger so the break is a surprise.

Follow Through

- FOLLOW-THROUGH enables the shooter to integrate, maintain and continue the shooting fundamentals before, during and after the shot.

Two Most Important Fundamentals of Handgun Shooting

- AIMING (sight alignment and sight picture)
- TRIGGER CONTROL

Firearms Range Instructions

- Eye protection
- Ear protection
- Ammunition (50 rounds will be used)
- Suggested Clothing:
  - Shirt with collar or crew neck
  - No sandals
  - No Shorts
  - Baseball Cap

Range Safety

- No handling of handguns until instructed to do so.
- Leave handgun in gun case or gun box.
- Ammunition should not be loose. 50 rounds required.
- Slide is locked back.
- Magazine is out of the pistol.
- Ejection port is facing up.
- Muzzle pointed Down range

At the Gun Range

- Muzzle is always pointed downrange.
- Finger is "indexed" and off trigger until ready to fire.
- Loading is done when instructed to do so.
- If there is a loading or fail to eject or fail to fire, raise non gun hand & observe gun safety rules.
- If a cease fire is called, immediately cease firing, keep handgun pointed in a safe position.

Shooting Qualification for CHL

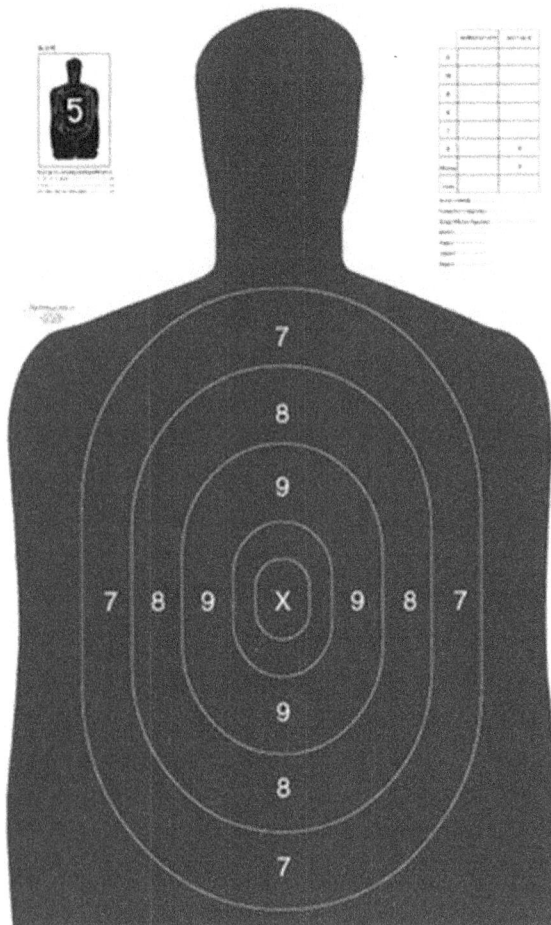

20 Rounds from 3 Yards

- Five rounds will be fired, one shot exercise, two seconds allowed for each shot.
- Ten rounds will be fired, two shot exercise, three seconds allowed for each shot.
- Five rounds will be fired, ten seconds for allowed for five shots

20 Rounds from 7 Yards

- The first five shots will be fired in ten seconds.
- The next five shots will be fired in two stages
  - Two shots will be fired in four seconds.
  - Three shots will be fired in six seconds.
- The next five shots at 7 yards will be fired as a one shot exercise. Three seconds allowed for each shot.
- The last five shots fired at the 7 yard line. The time will be fifteen seconds to shoot five rounds.

10 Rounds from 15 Yards

- The first five shots will be fired in two stages.
  - Two shots fired in six seconds.
  - Three shots fired in nine seconds.
- The last five rounds will be fired in fifteen seconds.

Scoring

- 8, 9 & 10 (x) Rings = 5 pts. Each
- 7 Ring = 4 pts.
- Outside the 7 Ring but on the target = 3 pts.
- Hole touching line goes to higher point
- 175 points needed to pass

Proper Handgun Storage

What is Safe Storage?

- Most would describe it as "Locking the handgun in a gun safe, or gun cabinet" or "Keeping the handgun separate from the ammunition."
- Restricting Access
- Safe storage goes much further and is a 24/7 responsibility.

Defining Safe Storage

- Goes beyond keeping the handgun locked in your house
- Is more than a storage device
- Applies anytime, anywhere
- Is not hiding your handgun
- Is a learned behavior
- Is a constant responsibility
- Can be the difference between life and death

Accessibility vs. Safekeeping

- Location
  - Workplace
  - Public Places
  - Home
  - Vehicle

Who Has Access to Your Home, Car or Office?

- Immediate family
- Extended family
- Friends of family
- Contractors
- Child care providers
- Unintended persons

Workplace

- Physical – Desk, office, locking drawer, gun safe, gun lock
- Job sites
- Company vehicle

Type of Employment

- Work attire
- Job duties
- Who do you work with, who has access to you or your belongings?
- Co-workers
- General public
- Children

Public Places

- Physical
  - Facility storage options
  - Vehicle/Parking
- Type of Location
  - Recreational – may have lockers
  - Restaurant – don't leave bag/purses at table unattended
- Hotel/Travel/Vacation
  - Use of safes (who has access?)
  - Valet parking (ensure handguns are not accessible in vehicles)
  - Use of luggage services (don't leave handguns in bags attended by hotel staff)
- Who has access to you or your belongings
  - Friends
  - Family
  - Children

Home

- Physical building
  - Location
  - Single family dwelling/Multi-family dwelling
- Storage Options
  - Locking drawer, gun safe, gun locks
- Who has access to your home?
  - Family
  - Friends
  - Children and/or their friends
  - Maintenance workers
  - Uninvited persons

Vehicle

- Car/Truck/RV/Motorcycle
- Locking drawer, box, safe
- Trunk, engine compartment, hidden compartment
- Parking location
- Who has access to your vehicle
- Repair persons
- Travel

Handguns Must Be Secured From

- Children
- Visitors
- Friends
- Relatives
- Maintenance Workers
- Persons we expect and persons we don't
- In short, EVERYONE but you!

Types of Safes

Biometric

Electronic Combo

Mechanical Lock

Gun Locks

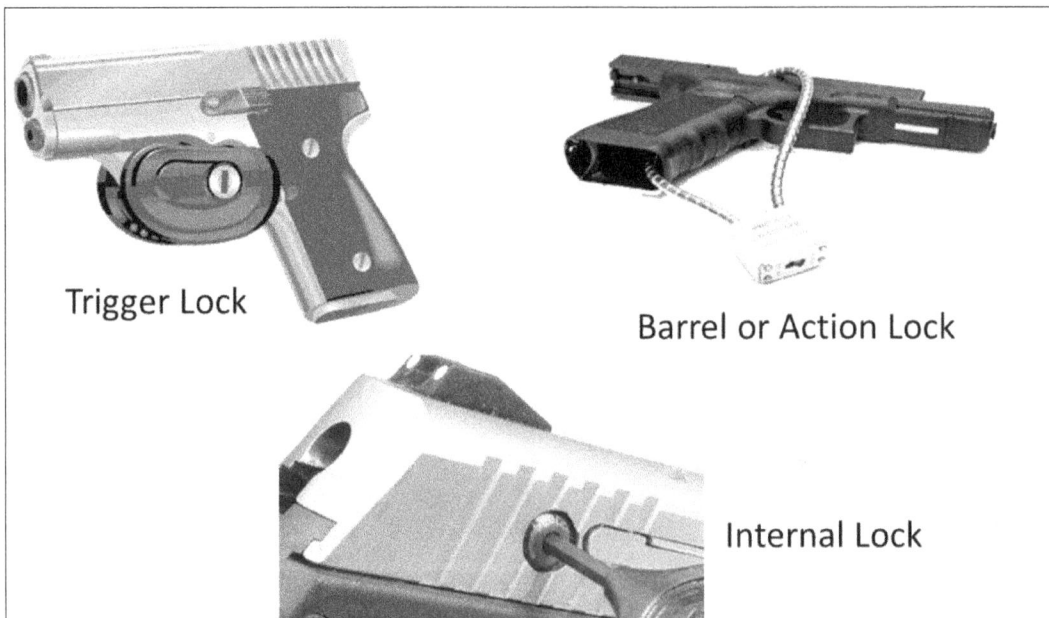

Trigger Lock

Barrel or Action Lock

Internal Lock

CONSIDERATIONS:

- Who has the combination/code/key?
- Is the locking device fixed or portable?
- How easy is it to breach the lock? (glass doors, for example)
- Can you get to it when you need it?

Making a Firearm Accessible to a Child

- "**Child**" means a person younger than 17 years of age.
- "**Readily dischargeable firearm**" means a firearm that is loaded with ammunition, whether or not a round is in the chamber.
- "**Secure**" means to take steps that a reasonable person would take to prevent access to a dischargeable firearm by a child, including but not limited to placing the firearm in a locked container or temporarily rendering the firearm inoperable by a trigger lock or other means.
- A person commits an offense if a child gains access to a readily dischargeable firearm and the person with criminal negligence:
  1. failed to secure the firearm; or
  2. left the firearm in a place to which the person knew or should have known the child would gain access
- It's a Class C misdemeanor
- It's a Class A misdemeanor if the child discharges the firearm and causes death or serious injury to himself or another person

Affirmable Defense to Prosecution of Child's Access

- The child was supervised by a person over 18 years of age and the child's access was for hunting, sporting or other lawful purposes.
- Consisted of lawful defense by the child of people or property.
- Was gained by entering property in violation of code
- Occurred during a time when the actor was engaged in an agricultural enterprise

Laws That Relate to the Use of Force and Deadly Force

Public Duty

- As a CHL Holder you have No legal duty to protect against or prevent a crime
- Deadly Force should only be used as a LAST RESORT.

Two Concepts by Which You Will Be Judged

- Was your action REASONABLE
- Was your action NECESSARY

Two types of Force

- NON-LETHAL FORCE – is force not known to cause serious bodily injury and/or death
- DEADLY FORCE (LETHAL) – is force that is intended, or known by the actor to cause, or in the manner of its use or intended use is capable of causing death or serious bodily injury.

DEADLY FORCE is to be used as a means of last resort, when all other means have failed and the fear for the loss of your life is immediate.

Less Lethal Defensive Items

- Verbal commands – "leave me alone", "Stay away from me."
- Impact weapons – flashlight, keys, pen.
- Other less-than-lethal weapons
- Handgun "IMPORTANT" – last resort

Wasp Spray

- Available anywhere
- Sprays up to 20-25 feet
- When sprayed in face, will give you a chance to get away

How Can You Know? – The AOJ Principle

How can you know the situation you were in was life-threatening and really involved danger of grave bodily harm or death?

Police are trained to answer this question by looking for three basic elements that must be present before the use of lethal force is justified.

- ABILITY
- OPPORTUNITY
- JEOPARDY

ABILITY means the other person has the power to cripple or kill you. This may or may not mean they have a weapon. It could exist:

- When a strong young person attacks a really old person
- When an adult attacks a child
- When a man attacks a woman
- When a healthy person attacks an injured person

OPPORTUNITY means the circumstances are such that the other person would be able to use his ability against you.

JEOPARDY means the other person's actions or words provide you with a reasonably-perceived belief that he Intends to kill you or cripple you.

An example of A & O, But Not J

A strong young man with a baseball bat (ability) is standing within a few feet of a man in a wheelchair (opportunity). Unless the young man either verbally or physically threatens to assault the other man, jeopardy is not present.

An Example of O & J, But Not A

A very irate little girl says, "I hate you! I'm going to kill you!" (jeopardy) She is standing right next to you, close enough to hit you with every ounce of her strength (opportunity). But she's only a little girl, and she doesn't have any weapons. Ability is not present.

An Example of A & J, But Not O

A small female has just testified in court against a male criminal who has been trained as a martial artist and who is physically much bigger and stronger than she is (ability). As the guilty verdict is read, the criminal rages to his feet and begins shouting and threatening to kill her right then and there (jeopardy). But he is restrained by handcuffs and by the bailiffs. Opportunity is not present.

Texas Castle Doctrine

- If a bad guy is <u>entering</u> or <u>attempting to enter</u> your occupied habitation, vehicle, or place of business or employment, the law will <u>presume</u> you acted reasonably in using deadly force.

- If a bad guy is <u>removing</u> or <u>attempting to remove</u> you from your occupied habitation, vehicle, or place of business or employment, the law will <u>presume</u> you acted reasonably in using deadly force.

HABITATION - Structure or vehicle adapted for overnight accommodations of persons. A detached garage, storeroom, shed, etc. is not part of your habitation. An RV or Motor Home is.

VEHICLE - Any device by which a person may be propelled in the normal course of commerce or transportation, except such devices as classified a "habitation."

ROAD RAGE - Many "road rage" incidents result in aggravated assault charges. If a person is in their car, they should only pull out a gun if they have a reasonable belief the other person's conduct constitutes an attempt to cause them immediate death or bodily injury.

Force is NOT JUSTIFIED in response to verbal provocation by itself.

Texas Stand Your Ground Law

A person who has a right to be present at the location where deadly force is used, is not required to retreat before using deadly force as long as they are:

- Not a trespasser
- Not engaged in criminal activity
- Not the initial aggressor

Legal Concepts

- **Theft** is the felonious taking and removing of personal property with intent to deprive the rightful owner of it
- **Burglary** is the unlawful entry of a 'structure' to commit a felony or a theft. Burglary is commonly known as a "break in," or, "breaking and entering." Robbery/Aggravated Robbery
- **Robbery** is the taking or attempting to take something of value from another person by use of force, threats or intimidation. It is committed in the presence of the victim.
- **Aggravated Robbery.** If a suspect makes a victim believe that he has a deadly weapon by showing a weapon, saying he has a weapon or displaying something that appears to be a weapon, it is aggravated robbery.

Law of Self Defense

Deadly Force is Legally Justified in Texas if You Reasonably Believe it is Immediately Necessary to prevent:

- Murder/Deadly Force
- Home Invasion/Carjacking
- Kidnapping
- Robbery/Aggravated Robbery
- Sexual Assault/Aggravated Sexual Assault

Law of Defense of Others

The same justification for defending yourself is justification for defending others, i.e. to prevent:

- Murder/Deadly Force
- Home Invasion/Carjacking
- Kidnapping
- Robbery/Aggravated Robbery
- Sexual Assault/Aggravated Sexual Assault

Just because you can, doesn't mean you have to. If you're not absolutely sure which one is the aggressor, which one is the good guy, best to call 911 and let Law Enforcement make the determination.

REMEMBER: As a CHL Holder, you have no legal duty to protect against, or prevent, a crime

If you're not absolutely sure which one is the aggressor, which one is the good guy, best to call 911 and let Law Enforcement make the determination.

Some Things to Consider:

- You may have to use force against someone you know.

- Bullets may not stop a perpetrator right away.

- Use of Force situation can be quite complex, requiring calm thinking under a lot of pressure.

- Advance Training such as **Refuse to be a Victim** and Advanced **Concealed Carry** are highly recommended.

Three Myths to Get Out of Your Thinking

- **Warning Shot** – a great way to get yourself killed (It may be legal to shoot somebody to defend yourself, but it's not legal to discharge a firearm in the city limits! Besides it WASTES ammo you may need!)
- **Shooting to Wound** – another great way to get yourself killed.
- **Citizen's Arrest** – we're not cops. We carry guns to defend ourselves, not to enforce the law.

Protection against Animals

- Texas Law specifically allows you to use deadly force against a dog or coyote who is attacking or has immediately attacked your: livestock, fowl or domestic animal.
- Texas Law allows for the killing of raccoons, opossums, skunks and other small mammals if they are damaging crops or your property.
- If you have reasonable fear of death or bodily injury, you can defend yourself from a "dangerous wild animal."

Protection of Your Property

Commits or Attempts to Commit…

Arson

Robbery/Burglary

Aggravated Robbery

Theft During the Nighttime

Criminal Mischief During the Nighttime

Nighttime is defined as 30 minutes after sunset and 30 minutes before sunrise.

Deadly Force is justified if you reasonably believe it is immediately necessary to prevent:
Arson, Burglary, Robbery, Aggravated Robbery, Theft During The Nighttime, Or Criminal Mischief During The Nighttime.

In addition, §9.42 of the Texas Penal Code provides if you reasonably believe deadly force is immediately necessary to prevent another's "fleeing immediately after committing burglary, robbery, aggravated robbery" from escaping with the property, and you reasonably believe that "the land or property cannot be protected or recovered by other means" or the use of "force other than deadly force" would expose you to "substantial risk of death or serious bodily injury," then you are legally justified to use deadly force.

Protection of Someone Else's Property

Same justification as protecting your own if:

- The third person has requested protection of their land or property
- You have a legal duty to protect the third person's property
- The third person's land or property is that of your spouse, parent, child, person residing with you or person under you care
- You reasonably believe the unlawful interference constitutes attempted or consummated theft of or criminal mischief to the tangible, movable property

Civil Liability

Two Independent Legal Systems

Criminal System — State v. You — You — Another v. You — Civil System

Texas Civil Practice and Remedies Code 83.001 – CIVIL IMMUNITY. A defendant who uses force or deadly force that is justified under Chapter 9 of the Penal Code is immune from civil liability for personal injury or death that results from the defendant's use of force or deadly force, as applicable.

This statute does not stop someone from suing you, but if you can get the District Attorney to file a Memorandum of Closure, indicating the investigation is complete and they found no fault with you, there's a good chance the Civil Suit will be dismissed in court.

Tort Suit – Law Suit in which someone believes they have suffered an injury or damage due to another person's actions or fault. They will try to prove one the following:

- Negligence – failure to exercise caution or reasonable care
- Gross Negligence – aggravated form of negligence; reckless disregard
- Intentional Act – willful engagement in the action causing harm

Laws That Relate to Weapons

Important Definitions

Handgun – Any firearm that is designed, made, or adapted to be fired with one hand - Penal Code § 46.01(5)

Premise (Public) Penal Code - §46.035(f)(3)

- A building or portion of a building
- Does not include any public or private driveway, street, sidewalk, or walkway, parking lot, parking garage or other parking area

Premises (Private) – §71.01. (a-2)

- For purposes of this section, "premises" includes real property and a recreational vehicle that is being used as living quarters, regardless of whether that use is temporary or permanent.
- So, your yard, pasture, feed lot, etc.

Important Texas Gun Information

- There is no waiting period for purchasing a firearm in the state of Texas.
- There is no state registration of firearms.
- If you have inherited or bought a gun from someone in Texas, there is no requirement to transfer the firearm into your name. (There is no "In Your Name" here.)
- In order to purchase a firearm in Texas, you will need a valid state-issued ID.
- With a Concealed Handgun License (CHL) you may carry a pistol or revolver on your person as long as it remains concealed.
- Long guns, such as rifles and shotguns, do not have to be concealed, but must be carried in a manner not calculated to cause alarm, and do not require a license.
- Open carry is not legal in Texas, but you may openly carry a gun:
  - On your own property
  - While participating in a sporting activity, such as being at a shooting range
  - While engaged in hunting

Keeping a Gun in Your Car

As of September 1, 2007 you can carry a loaded concealed handgun in your car without a CHL as long as:

- Handgun is not in plain sight (concealed)
- You're not prevented by law from owning a handgun
- You're not engaged in any crime other than a Class C misdemeanor
- You're not a member of a street gang

In September 2011, that law was extended to include your boat.

More Important Texas Gun Information

- Weapons such as machine guns, suppressors and short-barreled firearms are legal in the state of Texas. (As long as you meet Federal requirements)
- Texas has no restrictions on so-called "assault weapons" such as semi-automatic weapons like the AR15 rifle. (Modern Sporting Rifles)
- There is no limit on the number of rounds a magazine may hold.
- The only limit on magazines in Texas is the number of rounds you are physically able to cram into the thing and/or carry and/or afford.

Crimes Against Society Involving Firearms

- If a person intentionally discharges a firearm within the City Limits (small town) it's a Class C Misdemeanor
- If a person recklessly discharges a firearm inside the corporate limits of a city over 100,000 persons it's a Class A Misdemeanor

Disorderly Conduct With a Firearm

- Discharging a firearm in a public place other than a sport shooting range (Class B Misdemeanor)
- Discharging a firearm on or across a public road (Class C Misdemeanor)
- Displaying a firearm or other deadly weapon in a public place in a manner calculated to alarm (Class B Misdemeanor)

Crimes Against a Person Involving a Firearm

Deadly Conduct by Pointing a Firearm at a Person

- If a person recklessly points a firearm, whether loaded or unloaded, that places another person in imminent danger it is a Class A Misdemeanor (Don't forget the Number 1 Rule of Gun Safety).

Deadly Conduct by Shooting a Firearm at a Person

- If a person knowingly discharges a firearm at or in the direction of one or more persons it is a Third Degree Felony.

Deadly Conduct by Shooting a Firearm at a Building or Vehicle

- A person knowingly discharges a firearm at or in the direction of a habitation, building or vehicle that is occupied, or they don't know whether or not it is occupied, it is a Third Degree Felony.

Aggravated Assault With a Deadly Weapon

- Any physical contact or threat of contact which causes a person fear, offense, pain, bodily injury or serious bodily injury can be prosecuted as an assault.
- If a deadly weapon, such as a firearm (loaded or not), is used the crime is always considered "aggravated."
- Aggravated Assault is 2nd Degree Felony.
- It is a 1st Degree Felony if the victim is a member of one's family, a public servant, a security guard, or it is done in retaliation against a witness or reportee of a crime.

Manslaughter

- Reckless conduct that results in the death of another person.

Criminally Negligent Homicide

- A person causes the death of another by criminal negligence.

Murder

- A person intentionally or knowingly causes the death or another, or
- When intending to cause serious bodily injury commits a clearly dangerous act that causes the death of an individual.

Justification is available as a defense under Texas Law for each of these Misdemeanors or Felonies

Licensed Handgun Carry

- Unconcealed handguns, loaded or unloaded, must be carried in a shoulder or belt holster.

Handgun Restraint

A well restrained handgun

- Will generally not fall from the holster during movement or activity of the person.
- Is not easily removed by someone other than the person carrying the handgun.
- Is still readily available by the person carrying the handgun.

Holsters

There are various types of holsters.

- Some only encompass a portion of the handgun.
- Some encompass the entire handgun.
- Some have a single means for restraining, while others have multiple means of restraining the handgun.

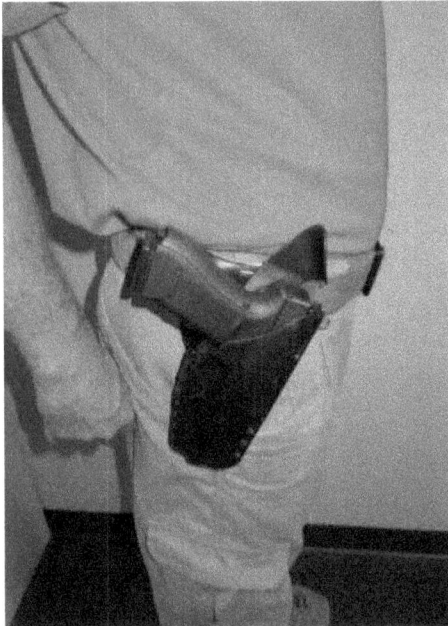

Belt Holster

Shoulder Holster

Types of Restraint Devices

- **Automatic** – Handgun will automatically be restrained when it is placed into the holster.

- **Manual** – Person must manually restrain the handgun in the holster.

Whether the shoulder or belt holster is equipped with a restraint device or without, it is critical for the person carrying to be familiar with the holster and be able to safely operate any restraint devices.

Places Where You Can't Carry Your Handgun

- On the premises of a school or school bus

- Premises does NOT include the parking lot

This sign does not prohibit the licensed carry of a handgun within the "DRUG FREE/GUN FREE School Zone." The Texas Law related to these zones is an escalation law that moves any conviction of a crime related to drugs or firearms to the next highest level of crime.

There is a Federal law that prohibits carry within 1,000 feet of a school any firearm that has been involved in "Interstate Commerce" (which is virtually all firearms). There are exceptions and among them being licensed by the state to carry. This law is virtually unenforceable, but there is always the possibility they would try. If you want to study it, you can Google 18 U.S.C. § 922 q.

- At a Polling place on the day of election or early voting

- At a Court House

At a race track where there is parimutuel betting

- In or into the secured area of an airport

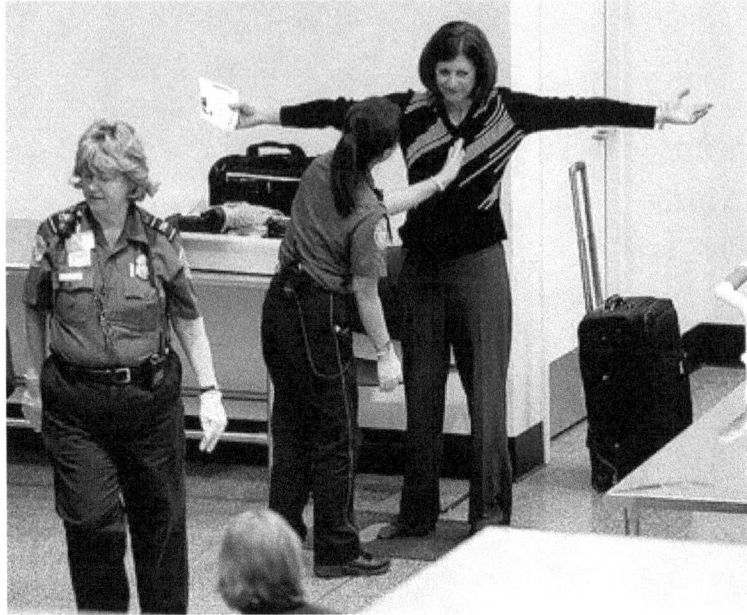

- It is a defense to prosecution if the actor possessed a handgun that he or she is licensed to carry at the security checkpoint of an airport, and exited the screening checkpoint for the secured area immediately upon completion of the required screening process and notification of possession of the handgun.

- The actor cannot be arrested for the sole offense of possessing a handgun that he or she is licensed to carry, unless a police officer gives the actor the opportunity to leave the area and he or she does not immediately comply.

- Within a 1,000 feet of an execution site on the day they're having an execution

Private Businesses

- Private businesses may post signs to indicate entry on the property with a handgun by a license holder is forbidden.
- Penal Code Section 30.06 provides the language to be included on signs to indicate license holders are forbidden to carry concealed.
- Penal Code Section 30.07 provides the language to be included on signs to indicate license holders are forbidden to open carry.
- Posting of both signs is an indication by the business that license holders are forbidden to carry concealed or openly

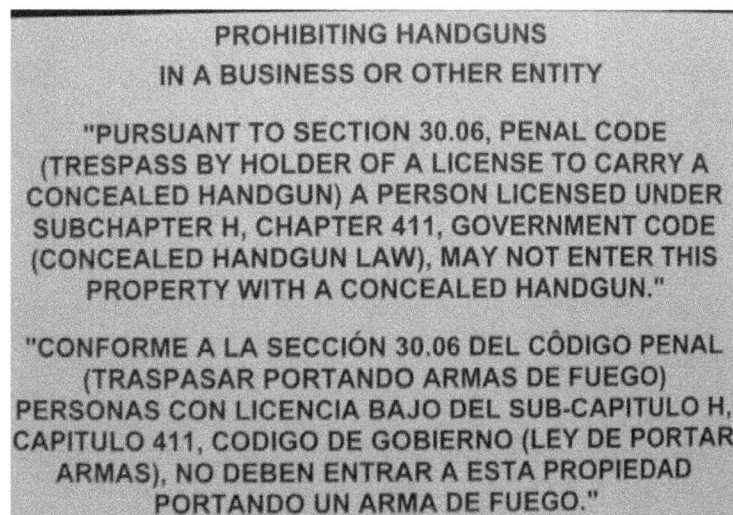

PROHIBITING HANDGUNS
IN A BUSINESS OR OTHER ENTITY

"PURSUANT TO SECTION 30.06, PENAL CODE
(TRESPASS BY HOLDER OF A LICENSE TO CARRY A
CONCEALED HANDGUN) A PERSON LICENSED UNDER
SUBCHAPTER H, CHAPTER 411, GOVERNMENT CODE
(CONCEALED HANDGUN LAW), MAY NOT ENTER THIS
PROPERTY WITH A CONCEALED HANDGUN."

"CONFORME A LA SECCIÓN 30.06 DEL CÓDIGO PENAL
(TRASPASAR PORTANDO ARMAS DE FUEGO)
PERSONAS CON LICENCIA BAJO DEL SUB-CAPITULO H,
CAPITULO 411, CODIGO DE GOBIERNO (LEY DE PORTAR
ARMAS), NO DEBEN ENTRAR A ESTA PROPIEDAD
PORTANDO UN ARMA DE FUEGO."

Property owned or leased by a State or Local Government entity cannot restrict you unless it is a place otherwise restricted (polling place, court house, etc.)

These signs have no meaning to you as a CHL Holder:

—NOTICE—

The unlicensed possession of a weapon on these premises is a felony with a maximum penalty of 10 years imprisonment and a fine not to exceed $10,000.

Texas Alcoholic Beverage Commission
P.O. Box 13127 Austin, Texas 78711-3127
Toll Free 1-888-THE-TABC (Voice/TDD)

You cannot carry in a bar that derives 51% or more of its revenue from the sale of alcohol for on-site consumption when they have the proper 51% sign posted.

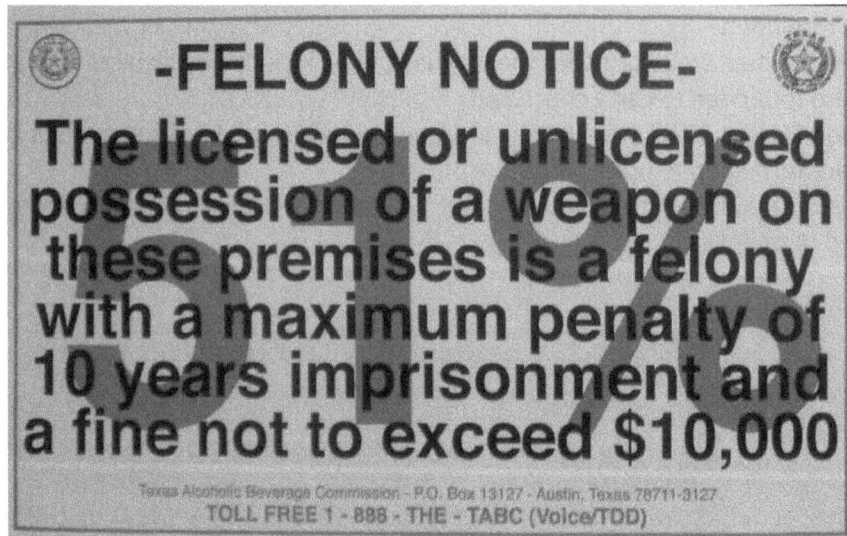

-FELONY NOTICE-
The licensed or unlicensed possession of a weapon on these premises is a felony with a maximum penalty of 10 years imprisonment and a fine not to exceed $10,000

Texas Alcoholic Beverage Commission - P.O. Box 13127 - Austin, Texas 78711-3127
TOLL FREE 1 - 888 - THE - TABC (Voice/TDD)

You cannot carry at a High School, Collegiate or Professional Sporting Event

You cannot carry at a Correctional Facility

You cannot carry on the property of the Federal Government (in most cases also includes the parking lot).

What About All Those Other Places You Think You Can't Carry?

- Churches
- Amusement Parks
- Hospitals
- Banks
- Restaurants
- Government Meetings

In the Law Book You'll See This as Places You Can't Carry:

(b)

(4) on the premises of a hospital or nursing home

(5) in an amusement park; or

(6) on the premises of a church, synagogue, or other place of religious worship.

(c) at any meeting of a governmental entity.

If You Turn a Few Pages Over You'll See:

(i) Subsections (b)(4), (b)(5), (b)(6), and (c) do not apply if the actor was not given effective notice under Section 30.06

Only if they have a 30.06 Sign

You Cannot Carry While Intoxicated

"Intoxicated" has the meaning assigned by Section 49.01, Penal Code, which says "Intoxicated" means:

    (A) not having the normal use of mental or physical faculties by reason of the introduction of alcohol, a controlled substance, a drug, a dangerous drug, a combination of two or more of those substances, or any other substance into the body; or

    (B) having an alcohol concentration of 0.08 or more.

Employers Can Prohibit On Premises

- 30.06 Sign
- Written or Verbal Notice
- Employee Handbook

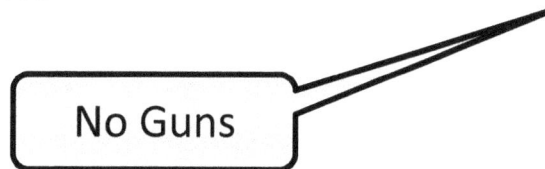

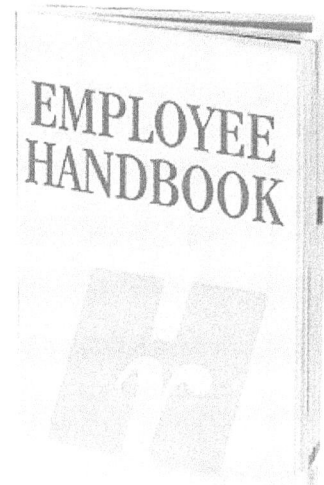

If it's only a restriction in the Handbook, you may be jeopardizing your job by carrying, but you are not breaking the law.

Employers Cannot Prohibit in Parking Lot (With Some Exceptions)

- Employees have the right to store a weapon in their vehicle while at work.
- Exceptions:
  - Vehicle owned or leased by a public or private employer
  - Schools
  - Private landowners leasing oil, gas, mineral rights
  - Chemical plants

Unlawful Possession of a Firearm

- Possession of a CHL does not explicitly authorize possession of a Firearm.
- For instance CHL holders could be ineligible to possess a firearm due to:
    - Mental or physical faculties
    - Violation of law
    - Administrative action

CHL Holders on College Campuses

Colleges and Universities may not prohibit a student enrolled at that institution who holds a license to carry a concealed handgun from transporting or storing a handgun in a locked, privately owned or leased vehicle:

1. on a street or driveway located on the campus of the institution; or
2. in a parking lot, parking garage, or other parking area located on the campus of the institution.

3. Senate Bill 11 (effective 8/1/2016) authorizes a license holder to carry a concealed handgun on or about the license holder's person while the license holder is on the campus of an institution of higher education or private or independent institution of higher education in this state.

4. Open carrying of handguns is still prohibited at these locations.

5. Community Colleges to follow Aug. 1, 2017.

Show Your CHL as ID

If a police officer or judge asks for your ID you must show them:

- Driver's License
- CHL

Technically, you don't have to show it if you're not carrying, but practically you ALWAYS want to show it. There's no downside to showing it, there may be an upside.

A Police Officer may disarm you if he feels you are a threat to him, others or yourself.

If he does not arrest you he must give your firearm back.

Conduct during a Traffic Stop

- Do not make quick movements, especially when the officer is present or approaching
- Have your hands on top of the steering wheel as much as possible
- If at night, turn on the dome light
- Open window(s) for communication
- Follow Instructions

Carrying on an Indian Reservation

- Depends upon the State's treaty with a specific tribe, the federal government's laws governing that tribe and the tribe's laws.
- If you cannot find this information, it's best to call the tribe in advance and ask their advice.
- Final option, if unable to confirm your ability to carry is to place the firearm in your trunk, unloaded during the duration of your travel within the reservation.

Carrying in National Parks

- The laws of the state in which the park is located apply

Federal Traveling Statute

This law is designed to protect you when traveling through a state that doesn't have reciprocity with Texas.

- Must be able to legally possess firearms at the start point and end point of your journey
- Firearms must not be readily accessible and unloaded
- Must be "traveling" through the state in question.
- This, of course does not apply to states that have CHL reciprocity with Texas.

Reciprocity (Map effective 8/23/15 – Subject to Change)

- States that have reciprocal agreements with Texas are listed on the DPS website.
- CHL holder must abide by the laws of the state in which they are traveling
- Reciprocity is not a blanket for all CHL holders.
  - Example: New Mexico does not allow anyone under 21 to carry.
  - Example: Some states will only honor Texas CHL if individual is a Texas resident

Non-Violent Dispute Resolution

Situational Awareness

- Pay attention to your physical surroundings
  - Consider safe parking location
  - Lighting conditions
  - Look before entering
  - Know where your exits are located
- Pay attention to people around you
  - Loitering, seasonally inappropriate attire
  - Conversation – words, tone
  - Actions by others
    - Clinched fists
    - Rapid or deep breathing
    - Excessive sweating
- Be safety conscious at all times
  - Lock car doors
  - Single lane at drive-thru (don't get boxed in)
  - ATM Transactions
  - Utilize the Buddy System (Safety in numbers)

Barriers Affecting Communications

- Environmental factors:
  - Noise (radio, traffic, other conversations)
  - Time of Day (day versus night)
  - Location (outside, inside)
- Language
- Physical/Emotional Factors
  - Hearing
  - Sight
  - Prior Interactions
  - Anger
  - Fear
- Cultural
  - Direct eye contact is expected or acceptable in some cultures, while in others it would be considered a sign of disrespect
  - Personal space or proximity varies among different cultures.

Communication Techniques

- Use of effective communication plays a key role in conflict resolution or conflict avoidance.
- Good verbal and non-verbal communication may help to avoid or diffuse a situation
- Being a better communicator may prevent the escalation of conflicts

Things to Consider

- Audience
- Age
- Culture
- Education/Profession

Verbal Communication

- Choice of words
- Jargon
- Positive/negative
- Offensive
- Tone
- Volume

Conflict Situations - Ego States

In 1964 Dr. Eric Berne wrote in his book "Games People Play" that we are each composed of three (3) separate "selves"

PARENT – ADULT – CHILD

At any given moment an individual in a social situation will exhibit one of these ego states; and, individuals can shift with varying degrees of readiness from one ego state to another.

PARENT EGO STATE

- Establishes rules, sets boundaries
- Provides training
- Directive
- Disciplinary
- Authoritative

CHILD EGO STATE

- Emotional – quick to anger
- May follow directions or may rebel
- Does not filter what he/she says

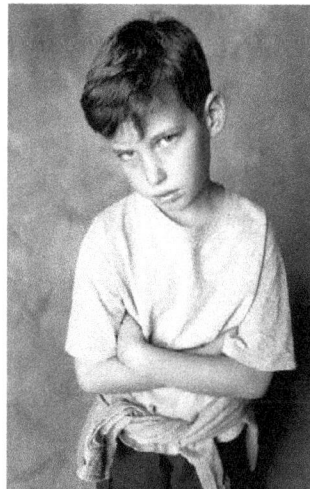

ADULT EGO STATE

- Does not dictate
- Uses good judgment, not emotions, to make decisions
- Carefully assesses the situation
- Shows respect for others and will compromise when necessary

According to Dr. Berne, the single best way to stop conflict is to speak in an **adult-to-adult** mode.

The only way to resolve conflict is to speak to a person in an **adult-to-adult** mode. This works to diffuse conflict by not allowing a person to get on the defensive and by letting them keep their self-respect and save face.

Practical Aspects of Concealed Carry

Note: This section contains information that is not part of the shortened Texas Concealed Handgun License curriculum that went into effect on September 1, 2013. Much of this material is covered in our Advanced Concealed Carry Classes.

Sheep, Wolves and Sheep Dogs

By: Lt. Col. Dave Grossman, U.S. Army (Ret.)

Honor never grows old, and honor rejoices the heart of age. It does so because honor is, finally, about defending those noble and worthy things that deserve defending, even if it comes at a high cost. In our time, that may mean social disapproval, public scorn, hardship, persecution, or as always, even death itself. The question remains: What is worth defending? What is worth dying for? What is worth living for?

William J. Bennett - in a lecture to the United States Naval Academy - November 24, 1997

One Vietnam veteran, an old retired colonel, once said this to me:

"Most of the people in our society are sheep. They are kind, gentle, productive creatures who can only hurt one another by accident." This is true. Remember, the murder rate is six per 100,000 per year, and the aggravated assault rate is four per 1,000 per year. What this means is that the vast majority of Americans are not inclined to hurt one another. Some estimates say that two million Americans are victims of violent crimes every year, a tragic, staggering number, perhaps an all-time record rate of violent crime. But there are almost 300 million Americans, which means that the odds of being a victim of violent crime is considerably less than one in a hundred on any given year. Furthermore, since many violent crimes are committed by repeat offenders, the actual number of violent citizens is considerably less than two million.

Thus there is a paradox, and we must grasp both ends of the situation: We may well be in the most violent times in history, but violence is still remarkably rare. This is because most citizens are kind, decent people who are not capable of hurting each other, except by accident or under extreme provocation. They are sheep.

I mean nothing negative by calling them sheep. To me it is like the pretty, blue robin's egg. Inside it is soft and gooey but someday it will grow into something wonderful. But the egg cannot survive without its hard blue shell. Police officers, soldiers, and other warriors are like that shell, and someday the civilization they protect will grow into something wonderful. For now, though, they need warriors to protect them from the predators.

"Then there are the wolves," the old war veteran said, "and the wolves feed on the sheep without mercy." Do you believe there are wolves out there who will feed on the flock without mercy? You better believe it. There are evil men in this world and they are capable of evil deeds. The moment you forget that or pretend it is not so, you become a sheep. There is no safety in denial.

"Then there are sheepdogs," he went on, "and I'm a sheepdog. I live to protect the flock and confront the wolf."

If you have no capacity for violence then you are a healthy productive citizen, a sheep. If you have a capacity for violence and no empathy for your fellow citizens, then you have defined an aggressive sociopath, a wolf. But what if you have a capacity for violence, and a deep love for your fellow citizens? What do you have then? A sheepdog, a warrior, someone who is walking the hero's path. Someone who can walk into the heart of darkness, into the universal human phobia, and walk out unscathed

Let me expand on this old soldier's excellent model of the sheep, wolves, and sheepdogs. We know that the sheep live in denial, that is what makes them sheep. They do not want to believe that there is evil in the world. They can accept the fact that fires can happen, which is why they want fire extinguishers, fire sprinklers, fire alarms and fire exits throughout their kids' schools.

But many of them are outraged at the idea of putting an armed police officer in their kid's school. Our children are thousands of times more likely to be killed or seriously injured by school violence than fire, but the sheep's only response to the possibility of violence is denial. The idea of someone coming to kill or harm their child is just too hard, and so they choose the path of denial.

The sheep generally do not like the sheepdog. He looks a lot like the wolf. He has fangs and the capacity for violence. The difference, though, is that the sheepdog must not, cannot and will not ever harm the sheep. Any sheepdog who intentionally harms the lowliest little lamb will be punished and removed. The world cannot work any other way, at least not in a representative democracy or a republic such as ours.

Still, the sheepdog disturbs the sheep. He is a constant reminder that there are wolves in the land. They would prefer that he didn't tell them where to go, or give them traffic tickets, or stand at the ready in our airports in camouflage fatigues holding an M-16. The sheep would much rather have the sheepdog cash in his fangs, spray paint himself white, and go, "Baa."

Until the wolf shows up. Then the entire flock tries desperately to hide behind one lonely sheepdog.

The students, the victims, at Columbine High School were big, tough high school students, and under ordinary circumstances they would not have had the time of day for a police officer. They were not bad kids; they just had nothing to say to a cop. When the school was under attack, however, and SWAT teams were clearing the rooms and hallways, the officers had to physically peel those clinging, sobbing kids off of them. This is how the little lambs feel about their sheepdog when the wolf is at the door.

Look at what happened after September 11, 2001, when the wolf pounded hard on the door. Remember how America, more than ever before, felt differently about their law enforcement officers and military personnel? Remember how many times you heard the word hero?

Understand that there is nothing morally superior about being a sheepdog; it is just what you choose to be. Also understand that a sheepdog is a funny critter: He is always sniffing around out on the perimeter, checking the breeze, barking at things that go bump in the night, and yearning for a righteous battle. That is, the young sheepdogs yearn for a righteous battle. The old sheepdogs are a little older and wiser, but they move to the sound of the guns when needed right along with the young ones.

Here is how the sheep and the sheepdog think differently. The sheep pretend the wolf will never come, but the sheepdog lives for that day. After the attacks on September 11, 2001, most of the sheep, that is, most citizens in America said, "Thank God I wasn't on one of those planes." The sheepdogs, the warriors, said, "Dear God, I wish I could have been on one of those planes. Maybe I could have made a difference." When you are truly transformed into a warrior and have truly invested yourself into warriorhood, you want to be there. You want to be able to make a difference.

There is nothing morally superior about the sheepdog, the warrior, but he does have one real advantage. Only one. And that is that he is able to survive and thrive in an environment that destroys 98 percent of the population. There was research conducted a few years ago with individuals convicted of violent crimes. These cons were in prison for serious, predatory crimes of violence: assaults, murders and killing law enforcement officers. The vast majority said that they specifically targeted victims by body language: slumped walk, passive behavior and lack of awareness. They chose their victims like big cats do in Africa, when they select one out of the herd that is least able to protect itself.

Some people may be destined to be sheep and others might be genetically primed to be wolves or sheepdogs. But I believe that most people can choose which one they want to be, and I'm proud to say that more and more Americans are choosing to become sheepdogs.

Seven months after the attack on September 11, 2001, Todd Beamer was honored in his hometown of Cranbury, New Jersey. Todd, as you recall, was the man on Flight 93 over Pennsylvania who called on his cell phone to alert an operator from United Airlines about the hijacking. When he learned of the other three passenger planes that had been used as weapons, Todd dropped his phone and uttered the words, "Let's roll," which authorities believe was a signal to the other passengers to confront the terrorist hijackers. In one hour, a transformation occurred among the passengers—athletes, business people and parents—from sheep to sheepdogs, and together they fought the wolves, ultimately saving an unknown number of lives on the ground.

There is no safety for honest men except by believing all possible evil of evil men. ~Edmund Burke

Here is the point I like to emphasize, especially to the thousands of police officers and soldiers I speak to each year. In nature the sheep, real sheep, are born as sheep. Sheepdogs are born that way, and so are wolves. They didn't have a choice. But you are not a critter. As a human being, you can be whatever you want to be. It is a conscious, moral decision.

If you want to be a sheep, then you can be a sheep and that is okay, but you must understand the price you pay. When the wolf comes, you and your loved ones are going to die if there is not a sheepdog there

to protect you. If you want to be a wolf, you can be one, but the sheepdogs are going to hunt you down and you will never have rest, safety, trust or love. But if you want to be a sheepdog and walk the warrior's path, then you must make a conscious and moral decision every day to dedicate, equip and prepare yourself to thrive in that toxic, corrosive moment when the wolf comes knocking at the door.

For example, many officers carry their weapons in church. They are well concealed in ankle holsters, shoulder holsters or inside-the-belt holsters tucked into the small of their backs. Anytime you go to some form of religious service, there is a very good chance that a police officer in your congregation is carrying. You will never know if there is such an individual in your place of worship, until the wolf appears to massacre you and your loved ones.

I was training a group of police officers in Texas, and during the break, one officer asked his friend if he carried his weapon in church. The other cop replied, "I will never be caught without my gun in church." I asked why he felt so strongly about this, and he told me about a cop he knew who was at a church massacre in Ft. Worth, Texas, in 1999. In that incident, a mentally deranged individual came into the church and opened fire, gunning down fourteen people. He said that officer believed he could have saved every life that day if he had been carrying his gun. His own son was shot, and all he could do was throw himself on the boy's body and wait to die. That cop looked me in the eye and said, "Do you have any idea how hard it would be to live with yourself after that?"

Some individuals would be horrified if they knew this police officer was carrying a weapon in church. They might call him paranoid and would probably scorn him. Yet these same individuals would be enraged and would call for "heads to roll" if they found out that the airbags in their cars were defective or that the fire extinguisher and fire sprinklers in their kids' school did not work. They can accept the fact that fires and traffic accidents can happen and that there must be safeguards against them.

Their only response to the wolf, though, is denial, and all too often their response to the sheepdog is scorn and disdain. But the sheepdog quietly asks himself, "Do you have any idea how hard it would be to live with yourself if your loved ones were attacked and killed, and you had to stand there helplessly because you were unprepared for that day?"

It is denial that turns people into sheep. Sheep are psychologically destroyed by combat because their only defense is denial, which is counterproductive and destructive, resulting in fear, helplessness and horror when the wolf shows up.

Denial kills you twice. It kills you once, at your moment of truth when you are not physically prepared: you didn't bring your gun, you didn't train. Your only defense was wishful thinking. Hope is not a strategy. Denial kills you a second time because even if you do physically survive, you are psychologically shattered by your fear, helplessness and horror at your moment of truth.

Gavin de Becker puts it like this in Fear Less, his superb post-9/11 book, which should be required reading for anyone trying to come to terms with our current world situation: "... denial can be seductive, but it has an insidious side effect. For all the peace of mind deniers think they get by saying it isn't so, the fall they take when faced with new violence is all the more unsettling."

Denial is a save-now-pay-later scheme, a contract written entirely in small print, for in the long run, the denying person knows the truth on some level.

And so the warrior must strive to confront denial in all aspects of his life and prepare himself for the day when evil comes. If you are warrior who is legally authorized to carry a weapon, and you step outside without that weapon, then you become a sheep, pretending that the bad man will not come today. No one can be "on" 24/7, for a lifetime. Everyone needs down time. But if you are authorized to carry a weapon, and you walk outside without it, just take a deep breath, and say this to yourself ...

"Baa."

This business of being a sheep or a sheepdog is not a yes/no dichotomy. It is not an all-or-nothing, either/or choice. It is a matter of degrees, a continuum. On one end is an abject, head-in-the-sand sheep and on the other end is the ultimate warrior. Few people exist completely on one end or the other. Most of us live somewhere in between. Since 9/11, almost everyone in America took a step up that continuum, away from denial. The sheep took a few steps toward accepting and appreciating their warriors, and the warriors started taking their jobs more seriously. The degree to which you move up that continuum, away from sheephood and denial, is the degree to which you and your loved ones will survive, physically and psychologically at your moment of truth.

Awareness

In today's society so many people go around immersed in their cell phones, oblivious to what's going on around them. This makes them extremely vulnerable to predators.

White	Relaxed and unaware of surroundings
Yellow	Relaxed but alert to surroundings
Orange	Something looks wrong/heightened awareness
Red	Something is wrong/action
	Extreme panic/caught unaware

Consider these states of mental awareness. Most people are in the white mode, relaxed and unaware of their surroundings. Get in the habit of being in at least the yellow mode, where you are paying attention to what is going on around you. That way, if something looks wrong, you can heighten your awareness and if it is wrong, take action. You never want to get caught unaware, which will most likely result in panic and the inability to defend yourself.

The Tueller Drill

The Tueller Drill is a self-defense training exercise to prepare against a short-range knife attack when armed only with a holstered handgun.

Sergeant Dennis Tueller, of the Salt Lake City, Utah Police Department wondered how quickly an attacker with a knife could cover 21 feet (6.4 m), so he timed volunteers as they raced to stab the target. He determined that it could be done in 1.5 seconds. These results were first published as an article in SWAT magazine in 1983 and in a police training video by the same title, "How Close is Too Close?"

A defender with a gun has a dilemma. If he shoots too early, he risks being charged with murder. If he waits until the attacker is definitely within striking range so there is no question about motives, he risks injury and even death. The Tueller experiments quantified a "danger zone" where an attacker presented a clear threat.

We have conducted these drills and have determined that even when you're ready and expecting it, a determined attacker can close as much as 30 feet in the time it takes to draw and fire your gun.

So the key is to not allow a threat to get that close to you before being ready for action. Keep your eyes open for potential attackers, especially when you "sense" something is wrong.

Response Time

- The time it takes to perceive the threat, analyze the situation and decide to react is your total response time.
- This varies in individuals and depends on a number of factors, such as age, upbringing and training.
- Whatever your carry method, practice, practice, practice!
- When you practice drawing from your holster or other carry equipment, work on smoothness, not speed. With smoothness, speed will come, but the key is to develop your muscle memory so the action will be performed automatically when your emotions may otherwise cloud clear thinking.
- To avoid being a victim, you need to develop a rapid response time. This involves staying aware and practicing what to do when and if you detect a threat. Your response time will vary among individuals AND your carry gun won't just jump into your hand when you need it. Whatever your carry method, practice drawing your gun (unloaded, of course) until it becomes an automatic response. When you can, practice with a loaded gun on a range that allows it.

Aftermath of the Use of Force

- The use of force against another is a decision one should not enter into lightly.
- Use of force against another may have
  - Physiological Effects
  - Emotional Effects

Physiological Effects of Being Under Stress

- Loss of fine Motor (muscle) Skills or Control: Fine movements of the fingers and hands are *degraded most of all*. Under stress, you *greatly lose physical coordination* that you would normally have. When a defensive technique requires you to perform finely coordinated movements with your fingers, such as *locating and operating small buttons and levers*, that procedure will probably break down under combative stress. Thus you want to incorporate the larger, stronger muscular movements into your combat reloading, stances, movement, and shooting repertoire.

- Tunnel Vision: Under stress, *your attention will be focused on the source of danger* to the complete exclusion of everything else. You will not be aware of the danger to the *sides and rear* of you. This is why you must move your left to right or right to left, and look in/over your backside, periodically when practicing shooting. Shoot the threat(s); look; then, quickly to left, right; then over right shoulder; then, left shoulder.

- Auditory Exclusion: Under stress, *sounds will be blocked out because your concentration is so intense on the source of danger*. You will not be aware of instructions shouted at you by an adjacent companion, *nor* will you hear his shots. Your shots will sound distant and muffled. As in tunnel vision, twisting your head side to side helps in restoring auditory function as well as shouting any commands to source of danger.

- Skewed Perception of Time or Space–Time Distortion: Stress will distort your *perception of time and space*. Events will appear to take place more slowly or in slow motion, making you think you have more time than you do. Be aware of this. For instance, you may think you shot only three bullets, but actually shot more. Thus, if you think you shot only three rounds, multiply it by three and that is approximately how much <u>you fired under stress Space–Time Distortion</u>, 3 x 3 = 9, and thus your weapon is most likely out of ammunition. Reload not when you have to. Reload when there is a lull in the battle!

- Objects will appear *closer* than they actually are. Your recollection of distances and times may differ greatly from that of other witnesses, even when there is no attempt on anyone's part to be untruthful. Therefore <u>volunteer no information</u>, written or verbal, about a lethal confrontation which involves you *until you see your attorney*; Simply say "I don't know," and *you don't know*. Let the facts speak for themselves. Also, information provided by "eye–witnesses" is often wrong. The sudden stress placed them also under this element of Tachy–Psyche. You want a good 'expert witness' on guns and Tachy Psyche! Have this witness explain to your lawyer about this so he can do his best in court should it get that far. In the meantime, learn to Shut–Up! Yes! That is you and me!

Emotional Aftermath

It is not unusual, when experiencing any type of traumatic event, to experience these emotional phases:

- Denial – refusal to admit the incident
- Anger – resentment of incident directed at self/others
- Bargaining – wishing the incident had not happened
- Depression – often the longest phase but it depends on the person
- Acceptance – accept the incident and begin to get on with life.

Let's talk about the Who, What, When, Where and How of Concealed Carry

Who

The "who" is you. Before carrying a gun on your person, you must be absolutely sure it's for you. The big question is "Can I take a life to defend myself or someone else?" If the honest answer is "no" then don't carry a gun. A person with an evil nature would be able to detect any hesitancy on your part to use a gun to defend yourself against them and could probably easily take that gun away from you and use it on you.

What

A big question facing many Concealed Handgun License holders is "What kind of gun should I carry?"

If this is your car and it's in a ditch, which of these vehicles would you prefer to have to tow it out?

The obvious answer is the one on the right, right?

If you have a flat tire . . .

Which of these jacks would you prefer to use to change it?

If you need to drive a spike . . .

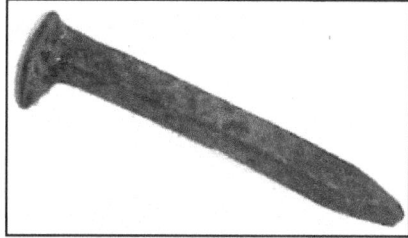

Which of these hammers is most suited for the task?

So, if you face this guy on a dark street and he's waving a gun in your face . . .

Which of these guns would you prefer to have to defend yourself?

The obvious answer is "the one on the right."

Yet so many people think of carrying a very small gun when they think of carrying concealed. Let's look at how that plays out in the real world.

What Actually Happens?

70% of Use of Force Shootings are:

- 3 Shots
- 3 Yards
- 3 Seconds
- 10% are 5-6 shots
- 20% involve 8-9 shots or more

How Do They Turn Out?

- Pocket Guns (5-shot 38s or less) – 50% chance of success
- Mid to Full Size guns – 80%-90% chance of success depending on your competence level

I don't know about you, but I want better odds than that.

Disadvantages to Small Guns

- Less power – smaller caliber & less muzzle velocity
- Fewer shots
- More recoil
- Harder to hold on to
- Less accurate

Three Things to Remember

- You're not carrying a gun just to carry a gun; you're carrying a gun to SAVE YOUR LIFE!
- "Carrying a concealed handgun is not supposed to be comfortable; it's supposed to be comforting." – Clint Smith
- Bad guys typically carry BIG GUNS (BG = BG)!

A Defensive Handgun Must Be 5 Things

- **Reliable** – must go "bang" every time trigger is pulled
- **Powerful** – must be able to stop an aggressor with one bullet
- **Handy** – you must be able to get to it quickly
- **It must be capable of rapid fire** – predators often roam in packs
- **Manageable** – must be easy to use

Get a good brand, a brand you can trust. And remember, expensive doesn't always mean better. Some of the guns we see malfunction most at the range are expensive brands (Colt, Kimber, Walther, to name a few).

Selecting the Right Gun

- **Ergonomics**
    - Is the grip angle and fit natural?
    - Can I reach all the controls?
    - Can I work the slide, slide release, magazine release?
- **Grip Size**
    - Perform the Middle Finger/Thumb Test to check for proper grip size
- **Trigger**
    - Perform a dry fire trigger test to make sure the trigger pull is not too difficult
- **Recoil**
    - Consider the caliber of the gun and the weight/size

Carry the Biggest Gun You can Comfortably Carry and Practice, Practice, Practice!

This photo shows the relative sizes between a .380, 9mm, .40 S&W and .45 ACP. It's not hard to figure out which one would be the best at stopping a threat.

Selecting the Right Ammunition

Full Metal Jacket   JHP – Defensive Rounds

Stopping Power

When it comes to making a bad guy stop what he's doing, there are several factors to consider.

- Foot pounds of energy at the target
- Size and Weight of the projectile
- Velocity in feet per second (FPS)
- Penetration – at least 9-10 inches
- Expansion – at least 1.5 times original size

Practically all modern defensive ammunition penetrates 9-10 inches and expands to 1.5 times it's original size. That's not the total picture when it comes to stopping power. A major factor is Energy on Target, which is measured in foot/pounds (ft./lbs.) which is computed with a formula based upon weight of the projectile and muzzle velocity in feet per second. Here's the formula if you want it:

$$E_k = \tfrac{1}{2}mv^2$$

Which can be simplified as E = (M x V^2) ÷ K where:

M is the weight of the projectile, in grains,
V is the velocity in feet per second and
E is the energy in foot pounds.

Based upon all the studies I've read and interviews with various individuals who have been shot, I've decided on a target of 400 ft./lbs. for the defensive ammunition I trust for my own personal defense.

Using the manufacturer's published data, I decided to conduct a study of the most effective ammunition I could find that is readily available for each handgun caliber. Here are the results:

Top .380 ACP Performers

Brand Name	Weight(Grs.)	Muzzle (fps)	Energy (ft./lbs.)
Winchester PDX-1	95	1000	211
Hornady Critical Defense	90	1000	200
Fiocchi Extrema	90	1000	200
Federal Premium HST	90	1000	200
Remington Ultimate Defense	102	940	200

Top 9mm Performers

Brand Name	Weight(Grs.)	Muzzle (fps)	Energy (ft./lbs.)
Speer Gold Dot	124+P	1220	410
Fiocchi Extrema	115	1250	400
Hornady American Gunner	124+P	1200	396
Winchester PDX-1	124+P	1200	396
Winchester Silvertip	115	1225	383

Top .40 S&W Performers

Brand Name	Weight(Grs.)	Muzzle (fps)	Energy (ft./lbs.)
Remington Terminal High Perf.	155	1205	499
Remington Ultimate Defense	180	1125	485
Remington Golden Saber	165	1150	485
Speer Gold Dot	165	1150	484
Fiocchi Extrema	155	1180	480

Top .45 ACP Performers

Brand Name	Weight(Grs.)	Muzzle (fps)	Energy (ft./lbs.)
Remington Golden Saber	185+P	1140	534
Speer Gold Dot	200+P	1080	518
Federal Premium Guard Dog	165	1140	476
Hornady Critical Duty	220+P	975	464
Winchester Silver Tip	230	920	432

Top .357 Sig Performers

Brand Name	Weight(Grs.)	Muzzle (fps)	Energy (ft/lbs)
Speer Gold Dot	125	1375	526
Winchester PDX-1/Silvertip	125	1350	506
Federal Premium HST	125	1350	506
Remington JHP	125	1350	506
Hornady Custom XTP	147	1225	490

Top 10mm Performers

Brand Name	Weight(Grs.)	Muzzle (fps)	Energy (ft/lbs)
Doubletap	150	1400	653
Buffalo Bore	180	1350	728
Winchester Silvertip	175	1290	649
Hornady Custom XTP	180	1180	556
Federal Premium HST	180	1030	424

Let's not forget the revolver calibers.

327 Federal Magnum Top Performers

Brand Name	Weight(Grs.)	Muzzle (fps)	Energy (ft/lbs)
Speer Gold Dot	100	1500	500
Buffalo Bore	100	1450	465
American Eagle JHP	125	1400	435
Jamison Brass	90	1465	429
Federal Premium	85	1400	370

.38 Special Top Performers

Brand Name	Weight(Grs.)	Muzzle (fps)	Energy (ft/lbs)
Fiocchi Extrema	125+P	1050	306
Hornady Critical Defense	110+P	1090	290
Remington Golden Saber	125+P	975	264
Winchester PDX-1	140+P	950	260
Federal Premium Hydra Shok	129 +P	950	258

Notice something about these .38 specials? They're all +P and they aren't all that great. Think about that when you're trusting your 5-round lightweight .38 Special for protection.

.357 Magnum Top Performers

Brand Name	Weight(Grs.)	Muzzle (fps)	Energy (ft./lbs.)
Black Hills	125	1500	625
Federal Premium Hydra Shok	140	1400	609
Fiocchi Extrema	125	1450	584
Winchester Silvertip	125	1450	583
Winchester Silvertip	145	1290	535

.44 Magnum Top Performers

Brand Name	Weight(Grs.)	Muzzle (fps)	Energy (ft./lbs.)
Winchester Dual Bond	240	1300	900
Federal Premium Hydra Shok	225	1280	818
CCI Blazer	240	1200	767
Winchester Silvertip	240	1180	741
Remington High Terminal Perf.	240	1180	741

How Do the Calibers Compare?

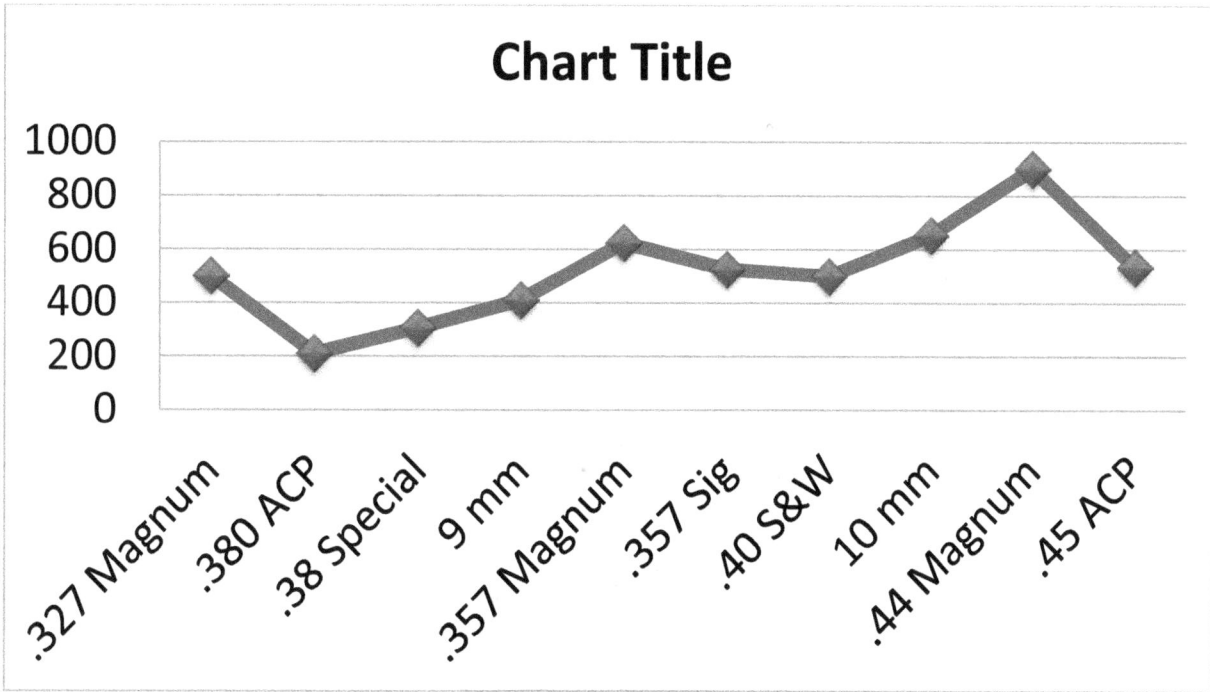

Chart Title

A line chart comparing energy (ft./lbs.) values on the y-axis (0 to 1000) for the following calibers: .327 Magnum (~500), .380 ACP (~200), .38 Special (~300), 9 mm (~400), .357 Magnum (~620), .357 Sig (~500), .40 S&W (~500), 10 mm (~650), .44 Magnum (~880), .45 ACP (~530).

It appears I can get my desired 400 ft./lbs. of energy from 9mm, .357 Magnum, .357 Sig, .40 S&W, 10mm, .44 Magnum, or .45 ACP.

Since I'm partial to .45 ACP, I have lots of ammo choices that will work. With a 9mm, I have to be pretty selective. Let's see, what if I have one of those highly-touted .380 powerhouses? Looks like the best I can do is a somewhere around 200 ft./lbs. That's less than HALF, what I've personally decided I'm comfortable with trusting for my own personal defense. Did I just pull that 400 ft./lbs. number out of the air? No, it came from a lot of judicious study.

CALIBER MATTERS!

You can do your own study, or read many of the studies out there. But whatever you decide, the next section is extremely important!

Most Important

- Know where to shoot
- Be able to hit where you are aiming
- Shoot until the threat is stopped

Where to Shoot

Law Enforcement and Military training for years went by the mantra "two to the chest, one to the head." Recent studies indicate that more than 80% of the time when Law Enforcement aims for the head with a handgun, they miss. It's not a large target and it's generally not stationary. Also just because you hit someone in the head, doesn't mean it's going to stop them. A deep brain shot, however, will.

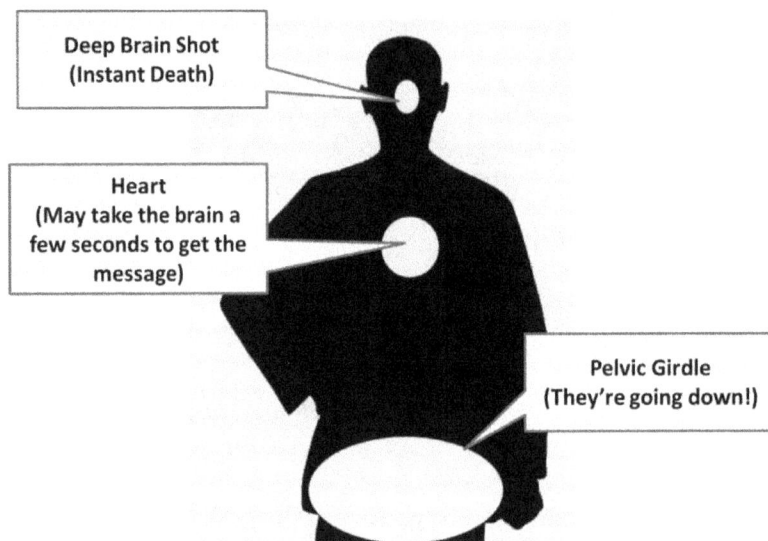

Deep Brain Shot
(Instant Death)

Heart
(May take the brain a
few seconds to get the
message)

Pelvic Girdle
(They're going down!)

Current training calls for shooting a couple of shots at the heart (much smaller area than "center mass") then concentrating your shots on the Pelvic Girdle area until the attacker goes down. The theory here is that if you shatter pelvis or femur or hip socket they're going down, giving you a chance to get away.

Real People Don't Have Circles on Them

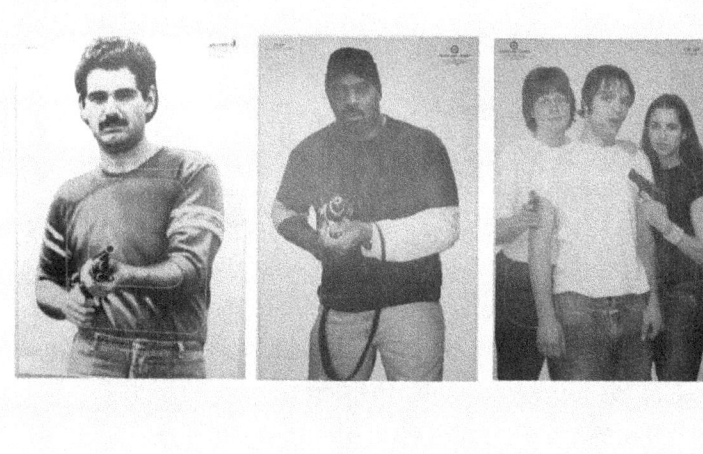

When you go to the range, try shooting at a variety of "bad guy" targets. Much more realistic than shooting at targets with circles on them.

When to Carry

We urge you to carry all the time. There is no way to predict when you might encounter a situation in which you may be called upon to defend your life or the lives of others. Random acts of violence can occur anywhere.

One of the heartbreaking stories regarding this is the story of Susanna Gratia Hupp, who owned a gun and typically carried it in her purse, but because of the laws in Texas at the time, left her gun in her car when dining with her parents at a Luby's Cafeteria in Killeen, Texas on October 16, 1991. That day a lunatic drove his truck through the front window of Luby's and began executing people. Susanna watched her mother and father killed, helpless to defend them because she had left her gun in her truck.

Don't be caught without your gun if you ever need it. And unless you have a magic crystal ball, how can you possibly know when that might be?

Where to Carry

There are very few places in Texas where you're not allowed to carry your concealed handgun:

- Schools
- Polling Places
- Court Houses
- Race Tracks
- High School, Collegiate or Professional Sporting Events
- Correctional Facility
- Outside an execution site when an execution is taking place
- In a bar that derives 51% or more of its revenue from the sale of alcohol for on-site consumption

- Post Office
- Federal Buildings
- Places that post a valid 30.06 sign

That's not a lot of places. Carry everywhere else.

Why Do We Carry?

- Under the 2nd amendment, citizens of the United States are granted the right to bear arms. The more of us that exercise that right, the harder it will be to take it away.
- You are responsible for your own safety, the first responder.
- 911 is after the fact and response times are often very long.
- In 1856, the U.S. Supreme Court ruled that local law enforcement had no duty to protect individuals, but only a general duty to enforce the laws. Source: South v Maryland, 59 US (HOW) 396, 15L.ED.433(1856)
- Police Department budgets are being slashed everywhere
- You can buy a gun without going through the FBI NICS Check.

How to Carry

There are numerous carry options. You'll have to find one that works for you. It will take making some concessions in your wardrobe, i.e. you may have to buy a size larger than normal. If you carry at your waist you'll need a good, strong gun belt.

Holsters come in inside the waistband (IWB) and outside the waistband (OWB) models as well as shoulder holsters and ankle holsters. Other carry options include fanny packs, day planners, purses and a variety of other somewhat creative methods.

Holsters we like include:

D.M. Bullard

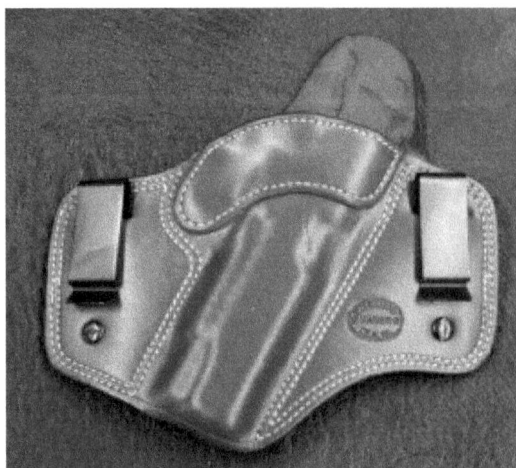

White Hat Holsters

N8^2 Tactical

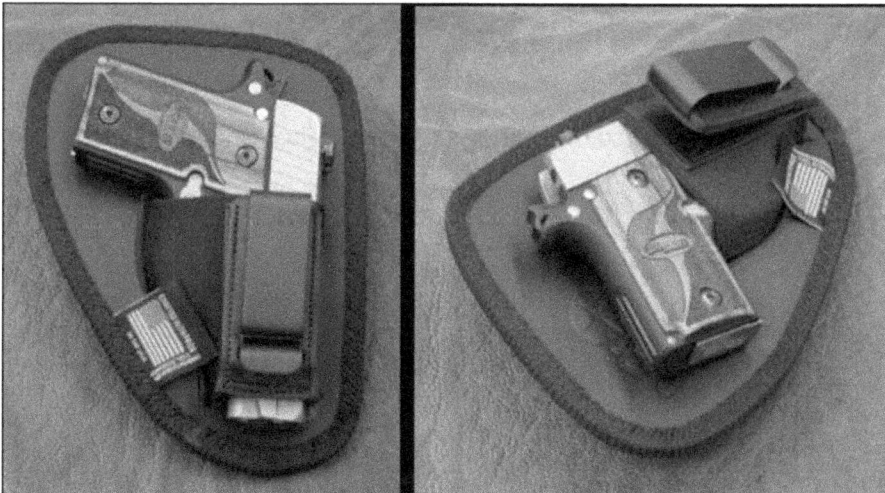

Gould & Goodrich Outside the Waistband

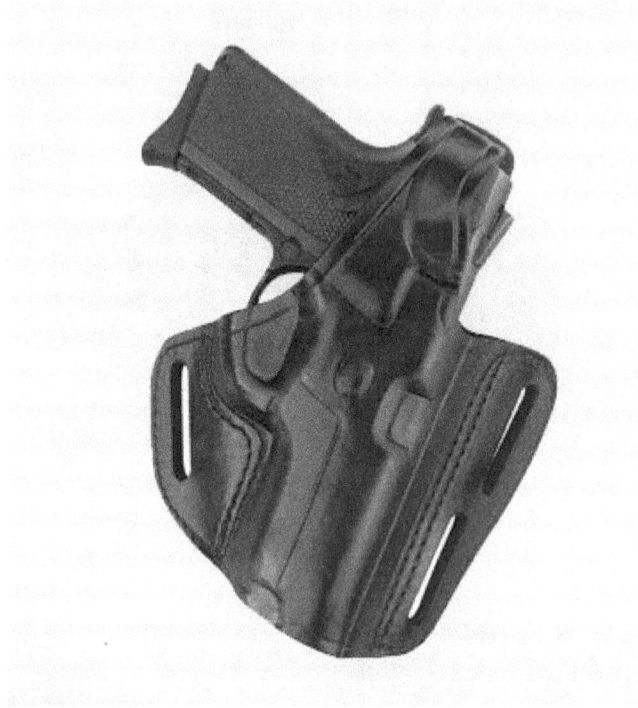

There are Concealed Carry purses of all sizes (just Google for them)

Resources for Ladies

These are just a few places where you can find concealed carry options for ladies:

- http://www.thewellarmedwoman.com
- http://www.naturallyconcealed.com
- http://www.mygunpurses.com
- http://flashbangholsters.publishpath.com
- http://www.armedinheels.com
- http://packingpretty.com

Pocket Holsters

If you're going to carry a gun in your pocket you'll need a holster designed to break up the outline of the gun and to keep it upright. The holster should also have a textured exterior designed to keep the holster in your pocket when your draw the gun.

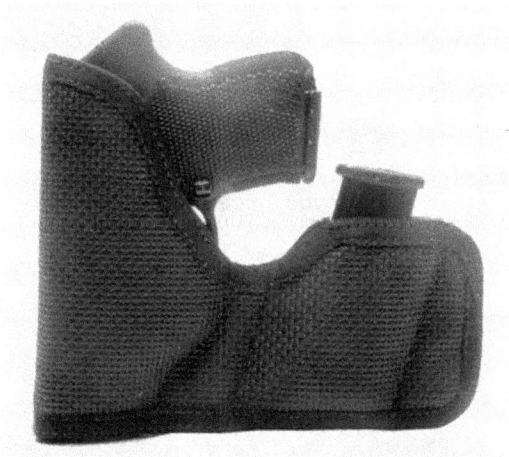

Spare Ammo

It's a good idea to carry spare ammo

- Your gun might malfunction
- "Bad Guys" often wear body armor
- "Bad Guys" are sometimes hopped up on drug
- You may encounter multiple assailants
- It's easy to carry spare ammo

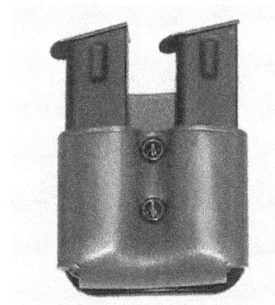

Don't Forget a Good Gun Belt

If you're going to wear a gun on your waist, a good gun belt is essential:

- It holds the gun securely
- It distributes the weight evenly

Vests

If you're going to wear a vest for concealed carry, don't use a tactical vest. We call them a "shoot me first" vest because it broadcasts the fact you're carrying a gun.

Instead, a nice casual or dress vest will work. You can get concealed carry vests with pockets that look just like a vest you'd get at Men's Wearhouse.

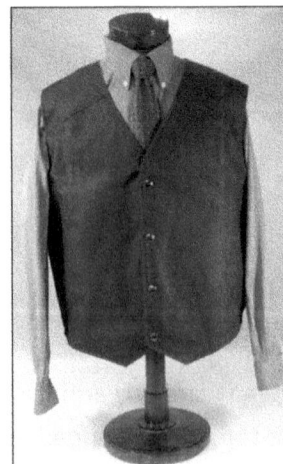

Ten Commandments of Concealed Carry

By Massad Ayoob

Note: This article appeared in the 2009 Concealed Carry Handguns annual.

Carrying a lethal weapon in public confers a grave power that carries with it great responsibilities. Those who lawfully engage in the practice realize that. Those who are considering "carrying" need to know what those experienced people know.

One - If You Carry, Always Carry

The criminal is the actor, and the armed citizen is the reactor. The typical violent criminal arms himself only when he intends to do something with it. He picks the time and place of the assault, and initiates the attack. Therefore, he doesn't need to worry about self-defense.

The armed citizen, the intended victim, does not know when or where that attack will come. Therefore, he or she must be constantly prepared and constantly vigilant. The "pistol-packer" learns to pick a comfortable holster and an appropriately sized handgun, and "dress around the firearm." After a few days, or a few weeks, it becomes second nature to wear it.

When the defender does not know when the attack will come, the only reasonable expectation of safety lies in being always armed.

Two - Don't Carry if You're Not Prepared to Use It

There is a great irony that attaches to the defensive firearm. When you analyze a great many defensive gun usages (DGUs) you discover that the great majority of the time, the protection weapon does its job with no blood being shed. Usually, the offender who is confronted with the prospect of being shot in self-defense either breaks off and runs or surrenders at gunpoint.

Its most important asset turns out to be its power to deter. The irony comes from the fact that its power to deter is drawn directly from its power to kill.

Understand that criminals do not fear guns. They are, after all, an armed subculture themselves. What they fear is the resolutely armed man or woman who points that gun at them. Criminals are predators, and their stock in trade is their ability to read people and recognize victims. They are very, very good at reading "body language" and determining another's intent to fight, or lack thereof. In short, you're not likely to bluff them.

If you carry a gun, you must be absolutely certain that you can use deadly force. The person who is hesitant or unwilling to do so will, in the moment of truth, communicate that vacillation to the hardened criminal they are attempting to hold at gunpoint. In such a case, it is quite likely that the offender will jump them, disarm them, and use the hesitant defenders' own weapons against them.

If, however, that same criminal realizes that he is facing a resolute person who will, in fact, shoot him if he takes one more transgressive step, he is most unlikely to take that step.

The irony: The person who is prepared to kill if he or she must, is the person who is least likely to have to do so.

Three - Don't Let the Gun Make You Reckless

Circa 1970, armed citizen Richard Davis invented the Second Chance vest, concealable body armor that for the first time could be worn constantly on duty, under the uniform, by any police officer. Some alarmists speculated that "being made bulletproof" would cause cops to become reckless. Those fears turned out to be totally unfounded. As any officer who has worn armor can attest, the vest is a constant reminder of danger and, if anything, makes its wearer more cautious.

It is much the same with concealed firearms in the hands of responsible private citizens. People unfamiliar with the practice fear that "the trigger will pull the finger," and armed citizens will go looking for a chance to exercise their deadly power. This, too, is a largely unfounded belief.

The collective experience of ordinary, law-abiding people who carry guns is that they don't feel a sudden urge to go into Central Park at three o'clock in the morning and troll for muggers. They learn that being armed, they are held to what the law calls "a higher standard of care" and are expected to avoid situations like traffic arguments that could escalate and, with a deadly weapon present, turn into killing situations.

Like an officer's body armor, the armed citizen's gun is a reminder of danger, a symbol of the need for caution. The late, great big game hunter and gun writer Finn Aagard once wrote, "Yet my pistol is more than just security. Like an Orthodox Jewish yarmulke or a Christian cross, it is a symbol of who I am, what I believe, and the moral standards by which I live."

Four - Get the License!

You'll hear some absolutists say, "No government has the right to permit me to carry a gun! I don't need no stinking permit! The Second Amendment is my license to carry!"

That is the sound of someone asking to go to jail. Like it or not, the laws of the land require, in 46 of the 50 states, a license to carry. In two states, there is no legal provision for the ordinary citizen to carry at all. Realize that things are not as we wish they were; things are as they are. If things were as we wish they would be, we wouldn't need to carry guns at all.

If you are diligent about studying carry license reciprocity, and about seeking non-resident carry permits in states that don't have reciprocity, you can become legal to carry in some forty or more states. It can get expensive, and it can get tiresome. However, allowing yourself to be made into a felon and being ramrodded through the courts is much more expensive and far more tiresome.

Bottom line: if you carry, make sure you carry legally.

Five - Know What You're Doing

You wouldn't drive an automobile without knowing the rules of the road. Do not keep or carry lethal weapons for defense without knowing the rules of engagement. It is a myth to believe that you can shoot anyone in your home. When Florida rescinded the requirement to retreat before using deadly force if attacked in public, the anti-gun Brady Center introduced a publicity campaign claiming that the new law allowed Floridians to shoot anyone who frightened them. This, of course, was blatantly untrue, but a great many people believed it to be so because "they heard it on TV" or "they saw it in the paper." Such dangerous misconceptions can cause the tragic death of people who don't deserve to be shot, and can get good people sent to prison.

It is the practitioner's responsibility to "learn the rules of the road" when they take the path toward armed self-defense. There are many firearms training schools, and at least one, the author's Lethal Force Institute, specializes in teaching the rules of engagement. Information is available under the LFI section at www.ayoob.com. It is wise to take local classes that emphasize the rules of "deadly force decision-making."

Similarly, a person who opens fire with a gun they don't know how to shoot is a danger to all. If you need the firearm for its intended purpose, you will be under extreme stress. Learn to shoot under pressure. Quick draw from concealment, safe holstering, proper tactics, and much more are on the curriculum if you are serious about defending yourself and your loved ones to the best of your ability.

Six - Concealed Means Concealed

A very few people carrying guns for the first time feel an irresistible urge to let others see that "they've got the power." First-time carriers and rookie cops, usually young in both cases, may fall into this trap. It is a practice to avoid for several reasons.

In most of this society, the only people the general public sees carrying guns in public are uniformed "protector figures," such as police officers and security guards. When they see someone not identifiable as such, who is carrying a lethal weapon, they tend to panic. This makes no friends among the voting public for the gun owners' rights movement—you do not make people into friends and sympathizers, by frightening them—and can lead to a panicky observer getting the wrong idea and reporting you to the police as a "man with a gun." This can lead to all sorts of unpleasant confrontations.

Moreover, a harasser who has picked you as his victim and knows you carry a gun can create a situation where there are no other witnesses present, and then make the false claim that you threatened him with the weapon. This is a very serious felony called Aggravated Assault. It is his word against yours. The fact that you are indeed carrying the gun he describes you pointing at him can make his lie more believable than your truth, to the ears of judge and jury.

MCRGO, Michigan Coalition of Responsible Gun Owners, is directly responsible for getting reform concealed carry legislation enacted in their state, and has been in the forefront of fighting for the rights of armed citizens in that state. MCRGO's Steve Dulan, in the organization's Weekly E'News of 6/23/08, had some cogent points to make on the topic of private citizens carrying handguns visibly in public:

"Open carry of firearms, subject to MCL 750.234d, it is legal to carry a visible pistol in public. MCRGO has not adopted an official position on this subject," wrote Dulan, who continued, "I agree with Ted Nugent and many others that it is a bad idea in almost every situation. Tactically, you are giving up the element of surprise should you face a deadly force situation. Furthermore, you run the risk of being called in to 9-1-1 as a 'man with a gun.' I have been on police ride-alongs when this call comes over the radio. It creates a very dangerous situation for all concerned. I do not carry openly. I have a CPL (Concealed Pistol License) and take care to choose a gun and holster that, along with appropriate clothing, allow me to keep my gun concealed unless/until I need it to save a life."

As cogent and valid as Steve Dulan's arguments are, it still makes sense to have legal open carry available as an emergency option. If the wind accidentally blows your coat open and reveals the gun, an open carry provision assures you have committed no crime. If someone who has not yet felt the need to get a concealed carry license suddenly begins getting death threats, open carry provides an emergency avenue of self-protection until the paperwork can be processed to acquire the license to carry the weapon discreetly out of sight.

Seven - Maximize Your Firearms Familiarity

The more you work with the firearm, the more reflexively skilled you will become in its emergency use and its safe handling. If your home defense shotgun is a Remington 870, then when you go claybird shooting or hunting, use an 870 pump gun with a barrel and choke appropriate for each task. If you are a target shooter who uses the 1911 pistol platform at bull's-eye matches and have become deeply familiar with it, it makes sense to acquire a concealable 1911 to use as your carry gun, so that the ingrained skill will directly transfer. If a double-action .44 Magnum is your hunting revolver, and another double-action revolver is your home defense gun, it makes sense to choose a carry-size revolver as your concealment handgun when you're out and about.

Consider training classes or competition shoots where your chosen defensive firearm is appropriate to the course of fire. This skill-building will translate to self-defense ability if your carry gun ever has to be used to protect innocent life and limb. If training ammunition is too expensive, consider a .22 conversion unit for your semiautomatic pistol or a .22 caliber revolver the same size as your defensive .38 or .357. The more trigger time you have with a similar gun, the more confidence and competence you'll have with the gun you carry, if you can't afford to practice as much as you'd like with the carry gun itself.

Eight - Understand the Fine Points

Every state has different laws insofar as where you can and can't carry a gun. It's your responsibility to know all the details. In one state, it may be against the law to carry a weapon in a posted "no-gun zone." In another, that sign may have no weight of law at all behind it. In a third, you may be asked to leave if your gun is spotted, and if you do not depart, you will be subject to arrest for Trespass After Warning.

In the state of New Hampshire, it is perfectly legal to carry your gun into a bar while you sit down and have a drink. If you do the same in Florida, it's an arrestable offense, though you're allowed to have a cocktail in a restaurant with a liquor license, so long as you're seated in a part of the establishment that earns less than 50% of its income from selling alcoholic beverages by the drink. In North Carolina, you can't even walk into a restaurant that has a liquor license, with a gun on. And, perhaps strangest of all, in the state of Virginia at this writing, it is illegal to enter a tavern with a concealed handgun, but perfectly legal to belly up to the bar and sip a whiskey while carrying a loaded handgun "open carry" fashion in an exposed holster!

A superb current compendium of gun laws in the 50 states can be found at www.handgunlaw.us. Review it frequently for possible changes.

Nine - Carry an Adequate Firearm

If you carry a single-shot, .22 Short caliber derringer, you will be considered armed with a deadly weapon in the eyes of the law. You will not, however, be adequately prepared to stop a predictable attack by multiple armed assailants. Most experts recommend a five-shot revolver as the absolute minimum in firepower, and the .380/9mm/.38SPL range as the minimum potency level in terms of handgun caliber.

It is a good idea to carry spare ammunition. Many people in their first gunfight have quickly found themselves soon clicking an empty gun. A firearm without spare ammunition is a temporary gun. Moreover, many malfunctions in semiautomatic pistols require a fresh (spare) magazine to rectify. Some fear that carrying spare ammo will make them look paranoid. They need to realize that those who don't like guns and dislike the people who carry them, will consider carrying the gun without spare ammunition to still be paranoid. It's an easy argument to win in court. Cops carry spare ammunition. So should you.

Carrying a second gun has saved the lives of many good people. When the primary weapon is hit by a criminal's bullet and rendered unshootable ... when it is knocked from the defender's hand, or snatched away by a criminal ... when the first gun runs out of ammo and there is no time to reload ... the list of reasons is endless. It suffices to remember the words of street-savvy Phil Engeldrum: "If you need to carry a gun, you probably need to carry two of them."

At the very least, once you've found a carry gun that works for your needs, it's a good idea to acquire another that's identical or at least very similar. If you have to use the first gun for self-defense, it will go into evidence for some time, and you want something you can immediately put on to protect yourself from vengeful cronies of the criminal you were forced to shoot. If the primary gun has to go in for repair, you don't want to be helpless or carrying something less satisfactory while you're waiting to get it back.

Ten - Use Common Sense

The gun carries with it the power of life and death. That power belongs only in the hands of responsible people who care about consequences, who are respectful of life and limb and human safety. Carrying a gun is a practice that is becoming increasingly common among ordinary American citizens. Common sense must always accompany it.

Recommended Reading

Books

A quick Google search on any of these books will turn up a source. In most cases, they can be found on Amazon.com. Others are available from Bloomfield Press.

- *In the Gravest Extreme* – Massad Ayoob
- *Gun Digest Book of Concealed Carry* – Massad Ayoob
- *Thank God I Had a Gun: True Accounts of Self-Defense* – Chris Bird
- *From Luby's to Legislature* – Suzanna Gratia Hupp
- *The Texas Gun Owner's Guide* – Alan Korwin and Georgene Lockwood
- *Gun Laws of America* – Alan Korwin With Michael P. Anthony

Periodicals

- *Shooting Times*
- *Shooting Times – Personal Defense Special Edition*
- *American Handgunner*
- *Handguns*
- *Personal Defense Handguns*

2015 Legislative Update

Summary of new laws passed in the 84th Regular Legislative Session that impact Concealed Handgun Licensing.

Open Carry

House Bill 910 *Effective: January 1, 2016*

Relating to the authority of a person who is licensed to carry a handgun to openly carry a holstered handgun; creating criminal offense.

General Information:

Authorizes individuals to obtain a license to openly carry a handgun in the same places that allow the licensed carrying of a concealed handgun with some exceptions. *(See "Exceptions" below for more information.)*

- Unconcealed handguns, loaded or unloaded, must be carried in a shoulder or belt holster.
- Individuals who hold a valid CHL may continue to carry with valid existing license.
- A separate license will not be required to open carry. No additional fee will be required.
- Individuals currently licensed will not be required to attend additional training. Training curriculum for new applicants will be updated to reflect the new training requirements related to the use of restraint holsters and methods to ensure the secure carrying of openly carried handguns. The new curriculum will be required for all classes beginning January 1, 2016.
- The eligibility criteria to obtain a license to carry do not change.
- The department will be updating website, forms and training materials to reference License to Carry (LTC) instead of Concealed Handgun License (CHL).
- Changes to the laminated license are being developed and will be implemented at a later date.

Signage:

- Private businesses may post signs to indicate entry on the property with a handgun by a license holder is forbidden.
- Penal Code Section 30.06 provides the language to be included on signs to indicate license holders are forbidden to carry concealed.
- Penal Code Section 30.07 provides the language to be included on signs to indicate license holders are forbidden to open carry.
- Posting of both signs is an indication by the business that license holders are forbidden to carry concealed or openly.

Exceptions:

- Open carry is not permitted by a license holder regardless of whether the handgun is holstered:
- on the premises of an institution of higher education or private or independent institution of higher education
- on any public or private driveway, street, sidewalk or walkway, parking lot, parking garage or other parking area of an institution of higher education or private or independent institution of higher education
- by an individual who is acting as a personal protection officer under Chapter 1702, Occupations Code and is not wearing a uniform

Campus Carry

Senate Bill 11 *Effective: August 1, 2016*

Relating to the carrying of handguns on the campuses of and certain other locations associated with institutions of higher education; providing a criminal penalty.

- Authorizes a license holder to carry a concealed handgun on or about the license holder's person while the license holder is on the campus of an institution of higher education or private or independent institution of higher education in this state. Open carrying of handguns is still prohibited at these locations.
- Authorizes an institution of higher education or private or independent institution of higher education in this state to establish rules, regulation, or other provisions concerning the storage of handguns in dormitories or other residential facilities that are owned or leased and operated by the institution and located on the campus of the institution.
- Requires the president or other chief executive officer of an institution of higher education in this state to establish reasonable rules, regulations, or other provisions regarding the carrying of concealed handguns by license holders on the campus or on specific premises located on the campus.
- Authorizes posting of a sign under Penal Code Section 30.06 with respect to any portion of a premises on which license holders may not carry.
- The effective date of this law for a public junior college is August 1, 2017

Various Other Changes

House Bill 554 *Effective: September 1, 2015*

Relating to a defense to prosecution for the offense of possessing or carrying a weapon in or into the secured area of an airport.

- Amends the Penal Code to add a defense to prosecution if the actor possessed a handgun that he or she is licensed to carry at the security checkpoint of an airport, and exited the screening checkpoint for the secured area immediately upon completion of the required screening process and notification of possession of the handgun.
- Adds the actor cannot be arrested for the sole offense of possessing a handgun that he or she is licensed to carry, unless a police officer gives the actor the opportunity to leave the area and he or she does not immediately comply.

House Bill 1376 *Effective; September 1, 2015*

Relating to the application of certain concealed handgun license laws to community supervision and corrections department officers and juvenile probation officers; reducing a fee.

- Allows supervision officers and juvenile probation officers to establish proof of proficiency by a sworn statement that indicates the person demonstrated proficiency with a firearm instructor licensed by the Texas Commission on Law Enforcement within the 12 month period preceding the application for the license to carry.
- This provision applies to supervision officers appointed or employed under Section 76.004, Government Code, to supervise defendants placed on community supervision.
- Reduces the fee for a license to carry to $25 for these individuals.
- Individuals applying under this special condition will be required to provide proof they are a supervision officer or juvenile probation officer.
- A new fee schedule will be posted on the department's website.

House Bill 2604 *Effective: September 1, 2015*

Relating to a concealed handgun license application that is submitted by a peace officer or a member of the state military forces.

- Exempts applicants who are active peace officers from the requirement to submit fingerprints.
- Repeals the provisions requiring a sworn statement from the head of the employing law enforcement agency regarding the applicant's conduct and proficiency.
- Regulatory Services Division (RSD) is in the process of updating the online application checklist. Until the online application is updated, peace officers may disregard the notations requiring fingerprints and the sworn statement from the head of their employing law enforcement agency.

- Updated application instructions for peace officers will be posted on the department's website upon the effective date of this law.

House Bill 2739 *Effective: September 1, 2015*

Relating to the use of a concealed handgun license as valid proof of personal identification.

- Amends the Business and Commerce Code to require businesses to accept a concealed handgun license (CHL) as a valid form of personal identification for access to goods, services, or facilities.
- Does not affect laws requiring a driver license to operate a motor vehicle.
- Does not effect the existing requirement to present a driver license when renting a car.
- Does not affect the type of identification required under federal law to access airport premises or to pass through airport security.

House Bill 3710 *Effective: September 1, 2015*

Relating to a voluntary contribution to the fund for veterans' assistance when applying for a concealed handgun license.

- Requires DPS to offer CHL applicants an opportunity to contribute money to the fund for veterans' assistance when applying for an original or renewal CHL license.
- The applicant will determine the amount of contribution.
- RSD is in the process of updating the online application to accept contributions. More information will be posted here when the option to contribute is available.

House Bill 3747 *Effective: June 16, 2015*

Relating to the issuance of a concealed handgun license to certain retired judicial officers.

- Authorizes retired federal judges to receive a discounted CHL in the same manner as a retired state judge.
- The reduced fee is $25. A new fee schedule will be posted on the department's website.

Senate Bill 273 *Effective September 1, 2015*

Relating to certain offenses relating to carrying concealed handguns on property owned or leased by a governmental entity; providing a civil penalty.

- Prohibits a state agency or political subdivision from posting signs stating where CHL holders are prohibited from carrying a concealed handgun on the premises, unless specifically prohibited by Texas Penal Code 46.03 and 46.035.
- Provides a civil penalty to a state agency or political subdivision if falsely notifying a CHL holder that entering or remaining on certain governmental premises, leased or owned, is illegal.

- Limits the scope of the governmental meeting prohibition by restricting it to the specific room or rooms in which the meeting is being held, and to public meetings for which notice is required under the Open Meetings Act.
- Provides an opportunity for the agency or subdivision to cure the violation within three business days of receipt of written notice from a citizen.
- Complaints of a violation are reported to the Attorney General Office.
- Provides the Attorney General must give notice to the agency or subdivision and provide an opportunity to cure the violation before a civil penalty is imposed.

TEXAS
LICENSE TO CARRY
A HANDGUN
LAWS

AND SELECTED STATUTES

2015 - 2016

issued by
Texas Department of Public Safety
Austin, Texas

CHL-16 *(revised)*

January 2016

This publication contains laws created and amended as the result of the passage of bills by the 84th Texas Legislature. The changes in the laws contained in this booklet are effective Sept. 1, 2015, unless otherwise noted. The statutes provided in this booklet have been downloaded from Texas Statutes Online at www.statutes.legis.state.tx.us.

DPS offers this material "as is." It makes no warranty as to the accuracy of the data, and users rely on the data entirely at their own risk. It is unable to aid in the conduct of research or offer legal advice. Please direct such requests to your local public library, the Legislative Reference Library, or an attorney as appropriate.

Handgun Licensing MSC 0245
Regulatory Services Division
Texas Department of Public Safety

Mail including payments:	*Mail without payments:*
P.O. Box 15888	P.O. Box 4087
Austin, Texas 78761-5888	Austin, Texas 78773-0245

(512) 424-7293

www.dps.texas.gov

Secured Email
www.dps.texas.gov/rsd/contact

Texas Administrative Code
http://texreg.sos.state.tx.us/public/readtac$ext.viewtac

Texas Legislature Online
www.capitol.state.tx.us

CONTENTS

GOVERNMENT CODE
Chapter 411 DEPARTMENT OF PUBLIC SAFETY OF THE STATE OF TEXAS
Subchapter D
Administrative Division

GC §411.047. REPORTING RELATED TO CONCEALED HANDGUN INCIDENTS.

(a) The department may maintain statistics on its website related to responses by law enforcement agencies to incidents in which a person licensed to carry a handgun under Subchapter H is convicted of an offense only if the offense is prohibited under Subchapter H or under Title 5, Chapter 29, Chapter 46, or Section 30.02, Penal Code.

(b) Such statistics shall be drawn and reported annually from the Department of Public Safety computerized criminal history file on persons 21 years of age and older and shall be compared in numerical and graphical format to all like offenses committed in the state for the reporting period as a percentage of the total of such reported offenses.

(c) The department by rule shall adopt procedures for local law enforcement to make reports to the department described by Subsection (a).

Last amended by Acts 2001, 77th Leg., ch. 1146, Sec. 1, eff. Sept. 1, 2001.

Subchapter H
License to Carry a Handgun

GC §411.171. DEFINITIONS. In this subchapter:

(1) Repealed by Acts 2013, 83rd Leg., R.S., Ch. 1302, Sec. 14(1), eff. June 14, 2013.

(2) "Chemically dependent person" means a person who frequently or repeatedly becomes intoxicated by excessive indulgence in alcohol or uses controlled substances or dangerous drugs so as to acquire a fixed habit and an involuntary tendency to become intoxicated or use those substances as often as the opportunity is presented.

Text of subdivision effective on Jan. 1, 2016

(3) Repealed by Acts 2015, 84th Leg., R.S., Ch. 437 , Sec. 50, eff. Jan. 1, 2016.

(4) "Convicted" means an adjudication of guilt or, except as provided in Section 411.1711, an order of deferred adjudication entered against a person by a court of competent jurisdiction whether or not the imposition of the sentence is subsequently probated and the person is discharged from community supervision. The term does not include an adjudication of guilt or an order of deferred adjudication that has been subsequently:

    (A) expunged;
    (B) pardoned under the authority of a state or federal official; or
    (C) otherwise vacated, set aside, annulled, invalidated, voided, or sealed under any state or federal law.

(4-a) "Federal judge" means:

    (A) a judge of a United States court of appeals;
    (B) a judge of a United States district court;
    (C) a judge of a United States bankruptcy court; or

(D) a magistrate judge of a United States district court.

(4-b) "State judge" means:

(A) the judge of an appellate court, a district court, or a county court at law of this state;

(B) an associate judge appointed under Chapter 201, Family Code; or

(C) a justice of the peace.

(5) "Handgun" has the meaning assigned by Section 46.01, Penal Code.

(6) "Intoxicated" has the meaning assigned by Section 49.01, Penal Code.

(7) "Qualified handgun instructor" means a person who is certified to instruct in the use of handguns by the department.

(8) Repealed by Acts 1999, 76th Leg., ch. 62, Sec. 9.02(a), eff. Sept. 1, 1999.

Added by Acts 1997, 75th Leg., ch. 165, Sec. 10.01(a), eff. Sept. 1, 1997. Amended by Acts 1999, 76th Leg., ch. 62, Sec. 9.01(a), 9.02(a), eff. Sept. 1, 1999.
Amended by:
Acts 2005, 79th Leg., Ch. 1084 (H.B. 1831), Sec. 1, eff. Sept. 1, 2005.
Acts 2007, 80th Leg., R.S., Ch. 594 (H.B. 41), Sec. 8, eff. Sept. 1, 2007.
Acts 2009, 81st Leg., R.S., Ch. 1146 (H.B. 2730), Sec. 6.06, eff. Sept.1, 2009.
Acts 2009, 81st Leg., R.S., Ch. 1146 (H.B. 2730), Sec. 11.02, eff. Sept. 1, 2009.
Acts 2009, 81st Leg., R.S., Ch. 1259 (H.B. 559), Sec. 2, eff. Sept. 1, 2009.
Acts 2013, 83rd Leg., R.S., Ch. 1302 (H.B. 3142), Sec. 14(1), eff. June 14, 2013.
Acts 2015, 84th Leg., R.S., Ch. 437 (H.B. 910), Sec. 50, eff. Jan. 1, 2016.

GC § 411.1711. CERTAIN EXEMPTIONS FROM CONVICTIONS.

A person is not convicted, as that term is defined by Section 411.171, if an order of deferred adjudication was entered against the person on a date not less than 10 years preceding the date of the person's application for a license under this subchapter unless the order of deferred adjudication was entered against the person for:

(1) a felony offense under:

(A) Title 5, Penal Code;

(B) Chapter 29, Penal Code;

(C) Section 25.07 or 25.072, Penal Code; or

(D) Section 30.02, Penal Code, if the offense is punishable under Subsection (c)(2) or (d) of that section; or

(2) an offense under the laws of another state if the offense contains elements that are substantially similar to the elements of an offense listed in Subdivision (1).

Last amended by Acts 2013, 83rd Leg., R.S., Ch. 96 (S.B. 743), Sec. 7, eff. Sept. 1, 2013.

GC §411.172. ELIGIBILITY.

Text of subsection effective on Jan. 1, 2016

(a) A person is eligible for a license to carry a handgun if the person:

(1) is a legal resident of this state for the six-month period preceding the date of application under this subchapter or is otherwise eligible for a license under Section 411.173(a);

(2) is at least 21 years of age;

(3) has not been convicted of a felony;

(4) is not charged with the commission of a Class A or Class B misdemeanor or equivalent offense, or of an offense under Section 42.01, Penal Code, or equivalent offense, or of a felony under an information or indictment;

(5) is not a fugitive from justice for a felony or a Class A or Class B misdemeanor or equivalent offense;

(6) is not a chemically dependent person;

(7) is not incapable of exercising sound judgment with respect to the proper use and storage of a handgun;

(8) has not, in the five years preceding the date of application, been convicted of a Class A or Class B misdemeanor or equivalent offense or of an offense under Section 42.01, Penal Code, or equivalent offense;

(9) is fully qualified under applicable federal and state law to purchase a handgun;

(10) has not been finally determined to be delinquent in making a child support payment administered or collected by the attorney general;

(11) has not been finally determined to be delinquent in the payment of a tax or other money collected by the comptroller, the tax collector of a political subdivision of the state, or any agency or subdivision of the state;

(12) is not currently restricted under a court protective order or subject to a restraining order affecting the spousal relationship, other than a restraining order solely affecting property interests;

(13) has not, in the 10 years preceding the date of application, been adjudicated as having engaged in delinquent conduct violating a penal law of the grade of felony; and

(14) has not made any material misrepresentation, or failed to disclose any material fact, in an application submitted pursuant to Section 411.174.

(b) For the purposes of this section, an offense under the laws of this state, another state, or the United States is:

(1) except as provided by Subsection (b-1), a felony if the offense, at the time the offense is committed:

(A) is designated by a law of this state as a felony;

(B) contains all the elements of an offense designated by a law of this state as a felony; or

(C) is punishable by confinement for one year or more in a penitentiary; and

(2) a Class A misdemeanor if the offense is not a felony and confinement in a jail other than a state jail felony facility is affixed as a possible punishment.

Text of subsection effective on Jan. 1, 2016

(b-1) An offense is not considered a felony for purposes of Subsection (b) if, at the time of a person's application for a license to carry a handgun, the offense:

(1) is not designated by a law of this state as a felony; and

(2) does not contain all the elements of any offense designated by a law of this state as a felony.

(c) An individual who has been convicted two times within the 10-year period preceding the date on which the person applies for a license of an offense of the grade of Class B misdemeanor or greater that involves the use of alcohol or a controlled substance as a statutory element of the offense is a chemically dependent person for purposes of this section and is not qualified to receive a license under this subchapter. This subsection does not preclude the disqualification of an individual for being a chemically dependent person if other evidence exists to show that the person is a chemically dependent person.

(d) For purposes of Subsection (a)(7), a person is incapable of exercising sound judgment with respect to the proper use and storage of a handgun if the person:

(1) has been diagnosed by a licensed physician as suffering from a psychiatric disorder or condition that causes or is likely to cause substantial impairment in judgment, mood, perception, impulse control, or intellectual ability;

(2) suffers from a psychiatric disorder or condition described by Subdivision (1) that:

(A) is in remission but is reasonably likely to redevelop at a future time; or

(B) requires continuous medical treatment to avoid redevelopment;

(3) has been diagnosed by a licensed physician, determined by a review board or similar authority, or declared by a court to be incompetent to manage the person's own affairs; or

(4) has entered in a criminal proceeding a plea of not guilty by reason of insanity.

(e) The following constitutes evidence that a person has a psychiatric disorder or condition described by Subsection (d)(1):

(1) involuntary psychiatric hospitalization;

(2) psychiatric hospitalization;

(3) inpatient or residential substance abuse treatment in the preceding five-year period;

(4) diagnosis in the preceding five-year period by a licensed physician that the person is dependent on alcohol, a controlled substance, or a similar substance; or

(5) diagnosis at any time by a licensed physician that the person suffers or has suffered from a psychiatric disorder or condition consisting of or relating to:

(A) schizophrenia or delusional disorder;

(B) bipolar disorder;

(C) chronic dementia, whether caused by illness, brain defect, or brain injury;

(D) dissociative identity disorder;

(E) intermittent explosive disorder; or

(F) antisocial personality disorder.

(f) Notwithstanding Subsection (d), a person who has previously been diagnosed as suffering from a psychiatric disorder or condition described by Subsection (d) or listed in Subsection (e) is not because of that disorder or condition incapable of exercising sound judgment with respect to the proper use and storage of a handgun if the person provides the department with a certificate from a licensed physician whose primary practice is in the field of psychiatry stating that the psychiatric disorder or condition is in remission and is not reasonably likely to develop at a future time.

Text of subsection effective on Jan. 1, 2016

(g) Notwithstanding Subsection (a)(2), a person who is at least 18 years of age but not yet 21 years of age is eligible for a license to carry a handgun if the person:

(1) is a member or veteran of the United States armed forces, including a member or veteran of the reserves or national guard;

(2) was discharged under honorable conditions, if discharged from the United States armed forces, reserves, or national guard; and

(3) meets the other eligibility requirements of Subsection (a) except for the minimum age required by federal law to purchase a handgun.

Text of subsection effective on Jan. 1, 2016

(h) The issuance of a license to carry a handgun to a person eligible under Subsection (g) does not affect the person's ability to purchase a handgun or ammunition under federal law.

Added by Acts 1997, 75th Leg., ch. 165, Sec. 10.01(a), eff. Sept. 1, 1997. Amended by Acts 1999, 76th Leg., ch. 62, Sec. 9.03(a), 9.04(a), eff. Sept. 1, 1999; Acts 2003, 78th Leg., ch. 255, Sec. 1, eff. Sept. 1, 2003.
Amended by:
Acts 2005, 79th Leg., Ch. 486 (H.B. 322), Sec. 1, eff. Sept. 1, 2005.
Acts 2009, 81st Leg., R.S., Ch. 1146 (H.B. 2730), Sec. 11.03, eff. Sept. 1, 2009.
Acts 2015, 84th Leg., R.S., Ch. 437 (H.B. 910), Sec. 17, eff. Jan. 1, 2016.

GC §411.173. NON-RESIDENT LICENSE.

(a) The department by rule shall establish a procedure for a person who meets the eligibility requirements of this subchapter other than the residency requirement established by Section 411.172(a)(1) to obtain a license under this subchapter if the person is a legal resident of another state or if the person relocates to this state with the intent to establish residency in this state. The procedure must include payment of a fee in an amount sufficient to recover the average cost to the department of obtaining a criminal history record check and investigation on a nonresident applicant. A license issued in accordance with the procedure established under this subsection:

(1) remains in effect until the license expires under Section 411.183; and

(2) may be renewed under Section 411.185.

(a-1) Repealed by Acts 2005, 79th Leg., Ch. 915, Sec. 4, eff. Sept. 1, 2005.

Text of subsection effective on Jan. 1, 2016

(b) The governor shall negotiate an agreement with any other state that provides for the issuance of a license to carry a handgun under which a license issued by the other state is recognized in this state or shall issue a proclamation that a license issued by the other state is recognized in this state if the attorney general of the State of Texas determines that a background check of each applicant for a license issued by that state is initiated by state or local authorities or an agent of the state or local authorities before the license is issued. For purposes of this subsection, "background check" means a search of the National Crime Information Center database and the Interstate Identification Index maintained by the Federal Bureau of Investigation.

(c) The attorney general of the State of Texas shall annually:

(1) submit a report to the governor, lieutenant governor, and speaker of the house of representatives listing the states the attorney general has determined qualify for recognition under Subsection (b); and

(2) review the statutes of states that the attorney general has determined do not qualify for recognition under Subsection (b) to determine the changes to their statutes that are necessary to qualify for recognition under that subsection.

(d) The attorney general of the State of Texas shall submit the report required by Subsection (c)(1) not later than Jan. 1 of each calendar year.

Added by Acts 1997, 75th Leg., ch. 165, Sec. 10.01(a), eff. Sept. 1, 1997. Amended by Acts 1999, 76th Leg., ch. 62, Sec. 9.05(a), eff. Sept. 1, 1999; Acts 2003, 78th Leg., ch. 255, Sec.

2, eff. Sept. 1, 2003; Acts 2003, 78th Leg., ch. 752, Sec. 1, eff. Sept. 1, 2003.
Amended by:
Acts 2005, 79th Leg., Ch. 915 (H.B. 225), Sec. 1, eff. Sept. 1, 2005.
Acts 2005, 79th Leg., Ch. 915 (H.B. 225), Sec. 2, eff. Sept. 1, 2005.
Acts 2005, 79th Leg., Ch. 915 (H.B. 225), Sec. 4, eff. Sept. 1, 2005.
Acts 2015, 84th Leg., R.S., Ch. 437 (H.B. 910), Sec. 18, eff. Jan. 1, 2016.

GC §411.174. APPLICATION.

Text of subsection effective on Jan. 1, 2016

(a) An applicant for a license to carry a handgun must submit to the director's
designee described by Section 411.176:
   (1) a completed application on a form provided by the department that requires
only the information listed in Subsection (b);
   (2) one or more photographs of the applicant that meet the requirements of the
department;
   (3) a certified copy of the applicant's birth certificate or certified proof of age;
   (4) proof of residency in this state;
   (5) two complete sets of legible and classifiable fingerprints of the applicant
taken by a person appropriately trained in recording fingerprints who is
employed by a law enforcement agency or by a private entity designated by
a law enforcement agency as an entity qualified to take fingerprints of an
applicant for a license under this subchapter;
   (6) a nonrefundable application and license fee of $140 paid to the
department;
   (7) evidence of handgun proficiency, in the form and manner required by the
department;
   (8) an affidavit signed by the applicant stating that the applicant:
      (A) has read and understands each provision of this subchapter that
creates an offense under the laws of this state and each provision of the
laws of this state related to use of deadly force; and
      (B) fulfills all the eligibility requirements listed under Section 411.172; and
   (9) a form executed by the applicant that authorizes the director to make an
inquiry into any noncriminal history records that are necessary to determine the
applicant's eligibility for a license under Section 411.172(a).
(b) An applicant must provide on the application a statement of the applicant's:
   (1) full name and place and date of birth;
   (2) race and sex;
   (3) residence and business addresses for the preceding five years;
   (4) hair and eye color;
   (5) height and weight;
   (6) driver's license number or identification certificate number issued by the
department;
   (7) criminal history record information of the type maintained by the
department under this chapter, including a list of offenses for which the
applicant was arrested, charged, or under an information or indictment and the
disposition of the offenses; and
   (8) history, if any, of treatment received by, commitment to, or residence in:
      (A) a drug or alcohol treatment center licensed to provide drug or alcohol
treatment under the laws of this state or another state, but only if the
treatment, commitment, or residence occurred during the preceding five

years; or

(B) a psychiatric hospital.

(b-1) The application must provide space for the applicant to:

(1) list any military service that may qualify the applicant to receive a license with a veteran's designation under Section 411.179(e); and

(2) include proof required by the department to determine the applicant's eligibility to receive that designation.

(c) The department shall distribute on request a copy of this subchapter and application materials.

(d) The department may not request or require an applicant to provide the applicant's social security number as part of an application under this section.

Added by Acts 1997, 75th Leg., ch. 165, Sec. 10.01(a), eff. Sept. 1, 1997. Amended by Acts 1999, 76th Leg., ch. 62, Sec. 9.06(a), eff. Sept. 1, 1999.
Amended by:
Acts 2005, 79th Leg., Ch. 486 (H.B. 322), Sec. 2, eff. Sept. 1, 2005.
Acts 2009, 81st Leg., R.S., Ch. 1146 (H.B. 2730), Sec. 11.04, eff. Sept. 1, 2009.
Acts 2013, 83rd Leg., R.S., Ch. 396 (S.B. 164), Sec. 1, eff. Sept.1, 2013.
Acts 2013, 83rd Leg., R.S., Ch. 665 (H.B. 1349), Sec. 2, eff. Jan. 1, 2014.
Acts 2015, 84th Leg., R.S., Ch. 437 (H.B. 910), Sec. 19, eff. Jan. 1, 2016.

GC §411.175. PROCEDURES FOR SUBMITTING FINGERPRINTS. The

department shall establish procedures for the submission of legible and classifiable fingerprints by an applicant for a license under this subchapter who:

(1) is required to submit those fingerprints to the department, including an applicant under Section 411.199, 411.1991, or 411.201; and

(2) resides in a county having a population of 46,000 or less and does not reside within a 25-mile radius of a facility with the capability to process digital or electronic fingerprints.

Added by Acts 2013, 83rd Leg., R.S., Ch. 874 (H.B. 698), Sec. 1, eff. Sept. 1, 2013.

GC §411.176. REVIEW OF APPLICATION MATERIALS.

(a) On receipt of application materials by the department at its Austin headquarters, the department shall conduct the appropriate criminal history record check of the applicant through its computerized criminal history system. Not later than the 30th day after the date the department receives the application materials, the department shall forward the materials to the director's designee in the geographical area of the applicant's residence so that the designee may conduct the investigation described by Subsection (b). For purposes of this section, the director's designee may be a noncommissioned employee of the department.

(b) The director's designee as needed shall conduct an additional criminal history record check of the applicant and an investigation of the applicant's local official records to verify the accuracy of the application materials.The director's designee may access any records necessary for purposes of this subsection. The scope of the record check and the investigation are at the sole discretion of the department, except that the director's designee shall complete the record check and investigation not later than the 60th day after the date the department receives the application materials. The department shall send a fingerprint card to the Federal Bureau of Investigation for a national criminal history check of the applicant. On completion of the investigation, the director's designee shall return all materials and the result of the investigation to the appropriate division of the department at its Austin headquarters.

(c) The director's designee may submit to the appropriate division of the department, at the department's Austin headquarters, along with the application materials a written recommendation for disapproval of the application, accompanied by an affidavit stating personal knowledge or naming persons with personal knowledge of a ground for denial under Section 411.172. The director's designee may also submit the application and the recommendation that the license be issued.

(d) On receipt at the department's Austin headquarters of the application materials and the result of the investigation by the director's designee, the department shall conduct any further record check or investigation the department determines is necessary if a question exists with respect to the accuracy of the application materials or the eligibility of the applicant, except that the department shall complete the record check and investigation not later than the 180th day after the date the department receives the application materials from the applicant.

Last amended by Acts 2009, 81st Leg., R.S., Ch. 1146 (H.B. 2730), Sec. 11.05, eff. Sept. 1, 2009.

GC §411.177. ISSUANCE OR DENIAL OF LICENSE.

Text of subsection effective on Jan. 1, 2016

(a) The department shall issue a license to carry a handgun to an applicant if the applicant meets all the eligibility requirements and submits all the application materials. The department shall administer the licensing procedures in good faith so that any applicant who meets all the eligibility requirements and submits all the application materials shall receive a license. The department may not deny an application on the basis of a capricious or arbitrary decision by the department.

(b) The department shall, not later than the 60th day after the date of the receipt by the director's designee of the completed application materials:

    (1) issue the license;

    (2) notify the applicant in writing that the application was denied:

        (A) on the grounds that the applicant failed to qualify under the criteria listed in Section 411.172;

        (B) based on the affidavit of the director's designee submitted to the department under Section 411.176(c); or

        (C) based on the affidavit of the qualified handgun instructor submitted to the department under Section 411.188(k); or

    (3) notify the applicant in writing that the department is unable to make a determination regarding the issuance or denial of a license to the applicant within the 60-day period prescribed by this subsection and include in that notification an explanation of the reason for the inability and an estimation of the amount of time the department will need to make the determination.

(c) Failure of the department to issue or deny a license for a period of more than 30 days after the department is required to act under Subsection (b) constitutes denial.

(d) A license issued under this subchapter is effective from the date of issuance.

Added by Acts 1997, 75th Leg., ch. 165, Sec. 10.01(a), eff. Sept. 1, 1997. Amended by Acts 1999, 76th Leg., ch. 62, Sec. 9.08(a), eff. Sept. 1, 1999.

Amended by:
Acts 2009, 81ˢᵗ Leg., R.S., Ch. 1146 (H.B. 2730), Sec. 11.06, eff. Sept. 1, 2009.
Acts 2013, 83ʳᵈ Leg., R.S., Ch. 1302 (H.B. 3142), Sec. 5, eff. June 14, 2013.
Acts 2015, 84ᵗʰ Leg., R.S., Ch. 437 (H.B. 910), Sec. 20, eff. Jan. 1, 2016.

GC §411.178. NOTICE TO LOCAL LAW ENFORCEMENT. On request of a local law enforcement agency, the department shall notify the agency of the licenses that have been issued to license holders who reside in the county in which the agency is located.

Last amended by Acts 1999, 76ᵗʰ Leg., ch. 1189, Sec. 14, eff. Sept. 1, 1999.

GC §411.179. FORM OF LICENSE.
(a) The department by rule shall adopt the form of the license. A license must include:
  (1) a number assigned to the license holder by the department;
  (2) a statement of the period for which the license is effective;
  (3) a color photograph of the license holder;
  (4) the license holder's full name, date of birth, hair and eye color, height, weight, and signature;
  (5) the license holder's residence address or, as provided by Subsection (d), the street address of the courthouse in which the license holder or license holder's spouse serves as a federal judge or the license holder serves as a state judge;
  (6) the number of a driver's license or an identification certificate issued to the license holder by the department; and
  (7) the designation "VETERAN" if required under Subsection (e).

Text of subsection as amended by Acts 2013, 83ʳᵈ Leg., R.S.,
Ch. 1302 (H.B. 3142), Sec. 6

(a) The department by rule shall adopt the form of the license. A license must include:
  (1) a number assigned to the license holder by the department;
  (2) a statement of the period for which the license is effective;
  (3)   a color photograph of the license holder;
  (4) the license holder's full name, date of birth, hair and eye color, height, weight, and signature;
  (5) the license holder's residence address or, as provided by Subsection (d), the street address of the courthouse in which the license holder or license holder's spouse serves as a federal judge or the license holder serves as a state judge; and
  (6) the number of a driver's license or an identification certificate issued to the license holder by the department.
(b) Repealed by Acts 2013, 83ʳᵈ Leg., R.S., Ch. 1302, Sec. 14(2), eff. June 14, 2013.
(c) In adopting the form of the license under Subsection (a), the department shall establish a procedure for the license of a qualified handgun instructor or of a judge, justice, prosecuting attorney, or assistant prosecuting attorney, as described by Section 46.15(a)(4) or (6), Penal Code, to indicate on the license the license holder's status as a qualified handgun instructor or as a judge, justice, district attorney, criminal district attorney, or county attorney. In establishing the

procedure, the department shall require sufficient documentary evidence to establish the license holder's status under this subsection.

(d) In adopting the form of the license under Subsection (a), the department shall establish a procedure for the license of a federal judge, a state judge, or the spouse of a federal judge or state judge to omit the license holder's residence address and to include, in lieu of that address, the street address of the courthouse in which the license holder or license holder's spouse serves as a federal judge or state judge. In establishing the procedure, the department shall require sufficient documentary evidence to establish the license holder's status as a federal judge, a state judge, or the spouse of a federal judge or state judge.

(e) In this subsection, "veteran" has the meaning assigned by Section 411.1951. The department shall include the designation "VETERAN" on the face of any original, duplicate, modified, or renewed license under this subchapter or on the reverse side of the license, as determined by the department, if the license is issued to a veteran who:

   (1) requests the designation; and

   (2) provides proof sufficient to the department of the veteran's military service and honorable discharge.

Added by Acts 1997, 75th Leg., ch. 165, Sec. 10.01(a), eff. Sept. 1, 1997.
Amended by:
Acts 2007, 80th Leg., R.S., Ch. 594 (H.B. 41), Sec. 9, eff. Sept. 1, 2007.
Acts 2007, 80th Leg., R.S., Ch. 1222 (H.B. 2300), Sec. 1, eff. June 15, 2007.
Acts 2009, 81st Leg., R.S., Ch. 87 (S.B. 1969), Sec. 27.001(25), eff. Sept. 1, 2009.
Acts 2009, 81st Leg., R.S., Ch. 87 (S.B. 1969), Sec. 27.002(6), eff. Sept. 1, 2009.
Acts 2009, 81st Leg., R.S., Ch. 316 (H.B. 598), Sec. 5, eff. Sept. 1, 2009.
Acts 2009, 81st Leg., R.S., Ch. 1146 (H.B. 2730), Sec. 11.07, eff. Sept. 1, 2009.
Acts 2013, 83rd Leg., R.S., Ch. 396 (S.B. 164), Sec. 2, eff. Sept. 1, 2013.
Acts 2013, 83rd Leg., R.S., Ch. 1302 (H.B. 3142), Sec. 6, eff. June 14, 2013.
Acts 2013, 83rd Leg., R.S., Ch. 1302 (H.B. 3142), Sec. 14(2), eff. June 14, 2013.
Acts 2015, 84th Leg., R.S., Ch. 1236 (S.B. 1296), Sec. 9.003, eff. Sept. 1, 2015.

GC §411.180. NOTIFICATION OF DENIAL, REVOCATION, OR SUSPENSION OF LICENSE; REVIEW.

(a) The department shall give written notice to each applicant for a handgun license of any denial, revocation, or suspension of that license. Not later than the 30th day after the notice is received by the applicant, according to the records of the department, the applicant or license holder may request a hearing on the denial, revocation, or suspension. The applicant must make a written request for a hearing addressed to the department at its Austin address. The request for hearing must reach the department in Austin prior to the 30th day after the date of receipt of the written notice. On receipt of a request for hearing from a license holder or applicant, the department shall promptly schedule a hearing in the appropriate justice court in the county of residence of the applicant or license holder. The justice court shall conduct a hearing to review the denial, revocation, or suspension of the license. In a proceeding under this section, a justice of the peace shall act as an administrative hearing officer. A hearing under this section is not subject to Chapter 2001 (Administrative Procedure Act). A district attorney or county attorney, the attorney general, or a designated member of the department may represent the department.

(b) The department, on receipt of a request for hearing, shall file the appropriate petition in the justice court selected for the hearing and send a copy of that petition to the applicant or license holder at the address contained in departmental records. A hearing under this section must be scheduled within 30 days of receipt of the request for a hearing. The hearing shall be held expeditiously but in no event more than 60 days after the date that the applicant or license holder requested the hearing. The date of the hearing may be reset on the motion of either party, by agreement of the parties, or by the court as necessary to accommodate the court's docket.

(c) The justice court shall determine if the denial, revocation, or suspension is supported by a preponderance of the evidence. Both the applicant or license holder and the department may present evidence. The court shall affirm the denial, revocation, or suspension if the court determines that denial, revocation, or suspension is supported by a preponderance of the evidence. If the court determines that the denial, revocation, or suspension is not supported by a preponderance of the evidence, the court shall order the department to immediately issue or return the license to the applicant or license holder.

(d) A proceeding under this section is subject to Chapter 105, Civil Practice and Remedies Code, relating to fees, expenses, and attorney's fees.

(e) A party adversely affected by the court's ruling following a hearing under this section may appeal the ruling by filing within 30 days after the ruling a petition in a county court at law in the county in which the applicant or license holder resides or, if there is no county court at law in the county, in the county court of the county. A person who appeals under this section must send by certified mail a copy of the person's petition, certified by the clerk of the court in which the petition is filed, to the appropriate division of the department at its Austin headquarters. The trial on appeal shall be a trial de novo without a jury. A district or county attorney or the attorney general may represent the department.

(f) A suspension of a license may not be probated.

(g) If an applicant or a license holder does not petition the justice court, a denial becomes final and a revocation or suspension takes effect on the 30th day after receipt of written notice.

(h) The department may use and introduce into evidence certified copies of governmental records to establish the existence of certain events that could result in the denial, revocation, or suspension of a license under this subchapter, including records regarding convictions, judicial findings regarding mental competency, judicial findings regarding chemical dependency, or other matters that may be established by governmental records that have been properly authenticated.

(i) This section does not apply to a suspension of a license under Section 85.022, Family Code, or Article 17.292, Code of Criminal Procedure.

Last amended by Acts 1999, 76th Leg., ch. 1412, Sec. 5, eff. Sept. 1, 1999.

GC §411.181. NOTICE OF CHANGE OF ADDRESS OR NAME.

(a) If a person who is a current license holder moves from any residence address stated on the license, if the name of the person is changed by marriage or otherwise, or if the person's status becomes inapplicable for purposes of the information required to be displayed on the license under Section 411.179, the person shall, not later than the 30th day after the date of the address, name, or status change, notify the department and provide the department with the number of the person's license and, as applicable, the person's:

(1) former and new addresses;

(2) former and new names; or

(3) former and new status.

(b) If the name of the license holder is changed by marriage or otherwise, or if the person's status becomes inapplicable as described by Subsection (a), the person shall apply for a duplicate license. The duplicate license must reflect the person's current name, residence address, and status.

(c) If a license holder moves from the address stated on the license, the person shall apply for a duplicate license.

(d) The department shall charge a license holder a fee of $25 for a duplicate license.

(e) The department shall make the forms available on request.

(f) On request of a local law enforcement agency, the department shall notify the agency of changes made under Subsection (a) by license holders who reside in the county in which the agency is located.

(g) If a license is lost, stolen, or destroyed, the license holder shall apply for a duplicate license not later than the 30th day after the date of the loss, theft, or destruction of the license.

(h) If a license holder is required under this section to apply for a duplicate license and the license expires not later than the 60th day after the date of the loss, theft, or destruction of the license, the applicant may renew the license with the modified information included on the new license. The applicant must pay only the nonrefundable renewal fee.

(i) A license holder whose application fee for a duplicate license under this section is dishonored or reversed may reapply for a duplicate license at any time, provided the application fee and a dishonored payment charge of $25 is paid by cashier's check or money order made payable to the "Texas Department of Public Safety."

Last amended by Acts 2009, 81st Leg., R.S., Ch. 1146 (H.B. 2730), Sec. 11.08, eff. Sept. 1, 2009.

GC §411.182. NOTICE.

(a) For the purpose of a notice required by this subchapter, the department may assume that the address currently reported to the department by the applicant or license holder is the correct address.

(b) A written notice meets the requirements under this subchapter if the notice is sent by certified mail to the current address reported by the applicant or license holder to the department.

(c) If a notice is returned to the department because the notice is not deliverable, the department may give notice by publication once in a newspaper of general interest in the county of the applicant's or license holder's last reported address. On the 31st day after the date the notice is published, the department may take the action proposed in the notice.

Added by Acts 1997, 75th Leg., ch. 165, Sec. 10.01(a), eff. Sept. 1, 1997.

GC §411.183. EXPIRATION.

(a) A license issued under this subchapter expires on the first birthday of the license holder occurring after the fourth anniversary of the date of issuance.

(b) A renewed license expires on the license holder's birthdate, five years after the date of the expiration of the previous license.

(c) A duplicate license expires on the date the license that was duplicated would have expired.

(d) A modified license expires on the date the license that was modified would have expired.

Last amended by Acts 2005, 79ᵗʰ Leg., Ch. 915 (H.B. 225), Sec. 3, eff. Sept. 1, 2005.

GC §411.185. LICENSE RENEWAL PROCEDURE.

(a) To renew a license, a license holder must, on or before the date the license expires, submit to the department by mail or, in accordance with the procedure adopted under Subsection (f), on the Internet:

  (1) a renewal application on a form provided by the department;

  (2) payment of a nonrefundable renewal fee as set by the department; and

  (3) the informational form described by Subsection (c) signed or electronically acknowledged by the applicant.

(b) The director by rule shall adopt a renewal application form requiring an update of the information on the original completed application. The director by rule shall set the renewal fee in an amount that is sufficient to cover the actual cost to the department to:

  (1) verify the information contained in the renewal application form;

  (2) conduct any necessary investigation concerning the license holder's continued eligibility to hold a license; and

  (3) issue the renewed license.

Text of subsection effective on Jan. 1, 2016

(c) The director by rule shall adopt an informational form that describes state law regarding the use of deadly force and the places where it is unlawful for the holder of a license issued under this subchapter to carry a handgun. An applicant for a renewed license must sign and return the informational form to the department by mail or acknowledge the form electronically on the Internet according to the procedure adopted under Subsection (f).

(d) Not later than the 60ᵗʰ day before the expiration date of the license, the department shall mail to each license holder a written notice of the expiration of the license, a renewal application form, and the informational form described by Subsection (c).

(e) The department shall renew the license of a license holder who meets all the eligibility requirements to continue to hold a license and submits all the renewal materials described by Subsection (a). Not later than the 45ᵗʰ day after receipt of the renewal materials, the department shall issue the renewed license or notify the license holder in writing that the department denied the license holder's renewal application.

(f) The director by rule shall adopt a procedure by which a license holder who satisfies the eligibility requirements to continue to hold a license may submit the renewal materials described by Subsection (a) by mail or on the Internet.

(g) The department may not request or require a license holder to provide the license holder's social security number to renew a license under this section.

Added by Acts 1997, 75ᵗʰ Leg., ch. 165, Sec. 10.01(a), eff. Sept. 1, 1997.
Amended by:
Acts 2007, 80ᵗʰ Leg., R.S., Ch. 694 (H.B. 1839), Sec. 1, eff. Sept. 1, 2007.
Acts 2009, 81ˢᵗ Leg., R.S., Ch. 1146 (H.B. 2730), Sec. 11.10, eff. Sept. 1, 2009.
Acts 2013, 83ʳᵈ Leg., R.S., Ch. 156 (S.B. 864), Sec. 1, eff. Sept. 1, 2013.
Acts 2013, 83ʳᵈ Leg., R.S., Ch. 665 (H.B. 1349), Sec. 3, eff. Jan. 1, 2014.
Acts 2013, 83ʳᵈ Leg., R.S., Ch. 1387 (H.B. 48), Sec. 1, eff. Sept. 1, 2013.
Acts 2015, 84ᵗʰ Leg., R.S., Ch. 437 (H.B. 910), Sec. 21, eff. Jan. 1, 2016.

Acts 2015, 84ᵗʰ Leg., R.S., Ch. 1236 (S.B. 1296), Sec. 9.004, eff. Sept. 1, 2015.
Acts 2015, 84ᵗʰ Leg., R.S., Ch. 1236 (S.B. 1296), Sec. 21.001(22), eff. Sept. 1, 2015.

GC §411.186. REVOCATION.

(a) The department shall revoke a license under this section if the license holder:
  (1) was not entitled to the license at the time it was issued;
  (2) made a material misrepresentation or failed to disclose a material fact in an application submitted under this subchapter;
  (3) subsequently becomes ineligible for a license under Section 411.172, unless the sole basis for the ineligibility is that the license holder is charged with the commission of a Class A or Class B misdemeanor or equivalent offense, or of an offense under Section 42.01, Penal Code, or equivalent offense, or of a felony under an information or indictment;
  (4) is convicted of an offense under Section 46.035, Penal Code;
  (5) is determined by the department to have engaged in conduct constituting a reason to suspend a license listed in Section 411.187(a) after the person's license has been previously suspended twice for the same reason; or
  (6) submits an application fee that is dishonored or reversed if the applicant fails to submit a cashier's check or money order made payable to the "Department of Public Safety of the State of Texas" in the amount of the dishonored or reversed fee, plus $25, within 30 days of being notified by the department that the fee was dishonored or reversed.

(b) If a peace officer believes a reason listed in Subsection (a) to revoke a license exists, the officer shall prepare an affidavit on a form provided by the department stating the reason for the revocation of the license and giving the department all of the information available to the officer at the time of the preparation of the form. The officer shall attach the officer's reports relating to the license holder to the form and send the form and attachments to the appropriate division of the department at its Austin headquarters not later than the fifth working day after the date the form is prepared. The officer shall send a copy of the form and the attachments to the license holder. If the license holder has not surrendered the license or the license was not seized as evidence, the license holder shall surrender the license to the appropriate division of the department not later than the 10ᵗʰ day after the date the license holder receives the notice of revocation from the department, unless the license holder requests a hearing from the department. The license holder may request that the justice court in the justice court precinct in which the license holder resides review the revocation as provided by Section 411.180. If a request is made for the justice court to review the revocation and hold a hearing, the license holder shall surrender the license on the date an order of revocation is entered by the justice court.

(c) A license holder whose license is revoked for a reason listed in Subsections (a)(1)(5) may reapply as a new applicant for the issuance of a license under this subchapter after the second anniversary of the date of the revocation if the cause for revocation does not exist on the date of the second anniversary. If the cause for revocation exists on the date of the second anniversary after the date of revocation, the license holder may not apply for a new license until the cause for revocation no longer exists and has not existed for a period of two years.

(d) A license holder whose license is revoked under Subsection (a)(6) may reapply for an original or renewed license at any time, provided the application fee and a dishonored payment charge of $25 is paid by cashier's check or money order made payable to the "Texas Department of Public Safety."

Last amended by Acts 2009, 81st Leg., R.S., Ch. 1146 (H.B. 2730), Sec. 11.11, eff. Sept. 1, 2009.

GC §411.187. SUSPENSION OF LICENSE.

(a) The department shall suspend a license under this section if the license holder:

(1) is charged with the commission of a Class A or Class B misdemeanor or equivalent offense, or of an offense under Section 42.01, Penal Code, or equivalent offense, or of a felony under an information or indictment;

(2) fails to notify the department of a change of address, name, or status as required by Section 411.181;

(3) commits an act of family violence and is the subject of an active protective order rendered under Title 4, Family Code; or

(4) is arrested for an offense involving family violence or an offense under Section 42.072, Penal Code, and is the subject of an order for emergency protection issued under Article 17.292, Code of Criminal Procedure.

(b) If a peace officer believes a reason listed in Subsection (a) to suspend a license exists, the officer shall prepare an affidavit on a form provided by the department stating the reason for the suspension of the license and giving the department all of the information available to the officer at the time of the preparation of the form. The officer shall attach the officer's reports relating to the license holder to the form and send the form and the attachments to the appropriate division of the department at its Austin headquarters not later than the fifth working day after the date the form is prepared. The officer shall send a copy of the form and the attachments to the license holder. If the license holder has not surrendered the license or the license was not seized as evidence, the license holder shall surrender the license to the appropriate division of the department not later than the 10th day after the date the license holder receives the notice of suspension from the department unless the license holder requests a hearing from the department. The license holder may request that the justice court in the justice court precinct in which the license holder resides review the suspension as provided by Section 411.180. If a request is made for the justice court to review the suspension and hold a hearing, the license holder shall surrender the license on the date an order of suspension is entered by the justice court.

(c) The department shall suspend a license under this section:

(1) for 30 days, if the person's license is subject to suspension for a reason listed in Subsection (a)(2), (3), or (4), except as provided by Subdivision (2);

(2) for not less than one year and not more than three years, if the person's license:

(A) is subject to suspension for a reason listed in Subsection (a), other than the reason listed in Subsection (a)(1); and

(B) has been previously suspended for the same reason;

(3) until dismissal of the charges, if the person's license is subject to suspension for the reason listed in Subsection (a)(1); or

(4) for the duration of or the period specified by:

(A) the protective order issued under Title 4, Family Code, if the person's license is subject to suspension for the reason listed in Subsection (a)(5); or

(B) the order for emergency protection issued under Article 17.292, Code of Criminal Procedure, if the person's license is subject to suspension for the reason listed in Subsection (a)(6).

Last amended by Acts 2013, 83ʳᵈ Leg., R.S., Ch. 1302 (H.B. 3142), Sec. 7, eff. June 14, 2013.

GC §411.1871. NOTICE OF SUSPENSION OR REVOCATION OF CERTAIN LICENSES. The department shall notify the Texas Commission on Law Enforcement if the department takes any action against the license of a person identified by the commission as a person certified under Section 1701.260, Occupations Code, including suspension or revocation.

Added by Acts 2013, 83ʳᵈ Leg., R.S., Ch. 655 (H.B. 1009), Sec. 4, eff. June 14, 2013.

GC §411.188. HANDGUN PROFICIENCY REQUIREMENT.
(a) The director by rule shall establish minimum standards for handgun proficiency and shall develop a course to teach handgun proficiency and examinations to measure handgun proficiency. The course to teach handgun proficiency is required for each person who seeks to obtain a license and must contain training sessions divided into two parts. One part of the course must be classroom instruction and the other part must be range instruction and an actual demonstration by the applicant of the applicant's ability to safely and proficiently use a handgun. An applicant must be able to demonstrate, at a minimum, the degree of proficiency that is required to effectively operate a handgun of.32 caliber or above. The department shall distribute the standards, course requirements, and examinations on request to any qualified handgun instructor.

Text of subsection effective on Jan. 1, 2016

(b) Only qualified handgun instructors may administer the classroom instruction part or the range instruction part of the handgun proficiency course. The classroom instruction part of the course must include not less than four hours and not more than six hours of instruction on:
   (1) the laws that relate to weapons and to the use of deadly force;
   (2) handgun use and safety, including use of restraint holsters and methods to ensure the secure carrying of openly carried handguns;
   (3) nonviolent dispute resolution; and
   (4) proper storage practices for handguns with an emphasis on storage practices that eliminate the possibility of accidental injury to a child.
(c) *Repealed by Acts 2013, 83ʳᵈ Leg., R.S., Ch. 156 (S.B. 864), Sec. 3, and Ch. 1387 (H.B. 48), Sec. 5, eff. Sept. 1, 2013.*
(d) Only a qualified handgun instructor may administer the proficiency examination to obtain a license. The proficiency examination must include:
   (1) a written section on the subjects listed in Subsection (b); and
   (2) a physical demonstration of proficiency in the use of one or more handguns and in handgun safety procedures.
(e) *Repealed by Acts 2013, 83ʳᵈ Leg., R.S., Ch. 1302, Sec. 14(4), eff. June 14, 2013.*
(f) The department shall develop and distribute directions and materials for course instruction, test administration, and recordkeeping. All test results shall be sent to the department, and the department shall maintain a record of the results.

Text of subsection effective on Jan. 1, 2016

(g) A person who wishes to obtain a license to carry a handgun must apply in person to a qualified handgun instructor to take the appropriate course in handgun proficiency and demonstrate handgun proficiency as required by the department.

(h) *Repealed by Acts 2013, 83ʳᵈ Leg., R.S., Ch. 1302, Sec. 14(4), eff. June 14, 2013.*

(i) A certified firearms instructor of the department may monitor any class or training presented by a qualified handgun instructor. A qualified handgun instructor shall cooperate with the department in the department's efforts to monitor the presentation of training by the qualified handgun instructor. A qualified handgun instructor shall make available for inspection to the department any and all records maintained by a qualified handgun instructor under this subchapter. The qualified handgun instructor shall keep a record of all information required by department rule.

(j) *Repealed by Acts 2015, 84ᵗʰ Leg., R.S., Ch. 1236 , Sec. 9.006, eff. Sept. 1, 2015.*

(k) A qualified handgun instructor may submit to the department a written recommendation for disapproval of the application for a license or modification of a license, accompanied by an affidavit stating personal knowledge or naming persons with personal knowledge of facts that lead the instructor to believe that an applicant does not possess the required handgun proficiency. The department may use a written recommendation submitted under this subsection as the basis for denial of a license only if the department determines that the recommendation is made in good faith and is supported by a preponderance of the evidence. The department shall make a determination under this subsection not later than the 45th day after the date the department receives the written recommendation. The 60-day period in which the department must take action under Section 411.177(b) is extended one day for each day a determination is pending under this subsection.

Added by Acts 1997, 75ᵗʰ Leg., ch. 165, Sec. 10.01(a) eff. Sept. 1, 1997. Amended by Acts 1999, 76ᵗʰ Leg., ch. 62, Sec. 9.11(a), eff. Sept. 1, 1999.
Amended by:
Acts 2009, 81ˢᵗ Leg., R.S., Ch. 1146 (H.B. 2730), Sec. 5.10, eff. Sept. 1, 2009.
Acts 2009, 81ˢᵗ Leg., R.S., Ch. 1146 (H.B. 2730), Sec. 11.13, eff. Sept. 1, 2009.
Acts 2013, 83ʳᵈ Leg., R.S., Ch. 156 (S.B. 864), Sec. 2, eff. Sept. 1, 2013.
Acts 2013, 83ʳᵈ Leg., R.S., Ch. 156 (S.B. 864), Sec. 3, eff. Sept. 1, 2013.
Acts 2013, 83ʳᵈ Leg., R.S., Ch. 1302 (H.B. 3142), Sec. 8, eff. June 14, 2013.
Acts 2013, 83ʳᵈ Leg., R.S., Ch. 1302 (H.B. 3142), Sec. 14(4), eff. June 14, 2013.
Acts 2013, 83ʳᵈ Leg., R.S., Ch. 1387 (H.B. 48), Sec. 2, eff. Sept. 1, 2013.
Acts 2013, 83ʳᵈ Leg., R.S., Ch. 1387 (H.B. 48), Sec. 5, eff. Sept. 1, 2013.
Acts 2015, 84ᵗʰ Leg., R.S., Ch. 437 (H.B. 910), Sec. 22, eff. Jan. 1, 2016.
Acts 2015, 84ᵗʰ Leg., R.S., Ch. 1236 (S.B. 1296), Sec. 9.005, eff. Sept. 1, 2015.
Acts 2015, 84ᵗʰ Leg., R.S., Ch. 1236 (S.B. 1296), Sec. 9.006, eff. Sept. 1, 2015.

GC §411.1881. EXEMPTION FROM INSTRUCTION FOR CERTAIN PERSONS.

(a) Notwithstanding any other provision of this subchapter, a person may not be required to complete the range instruction portion of a handgun proficiency course to obtain a license issued under this subchapter if the person:

  (1) is currently serving in or is honorably discharged from:

   (A) the army, navy, air force, coast guard, or marine corps of the United

States or an auxiliary service or reserve unit of one of those branches of the armed forces; or

(B) the Texas military forces, as defined by Section 437.001; and

(2) has, within the five years preceding the date of the person's application for the license, completed a course of training in handgun proficiency or familiarization as part of the person's service with the armed forces or Texas military forces.

(b) The director by rule shall adopt a procedure by which a license holder who is exempt under Subsection (a) from the range instruction portion of the handgun proficiency requirement may submit a form demonstrating the license holder's qualification for an exemption under that subsection. The form must provide sufficient information to allow the department to verify whether the license holder qualifies for the exemption.

Last amended by Acts 2013, 83ʳᵈ Leg., R.S., Ch. 1387 (H.B. 48), Sec. 3, eff. Sept. 1, 2013.

GC §411.1882. EVIDENCE OF HANDGUN PROFICIENCY FOR CERTAIN PERSONS.

(a) A person who is serving in this state as a judge or justice of a federal court, as an active judicial officer as defined by Section 411.201, as a district attorney, assistant district attorney, criminal district attorney, assistant criminal district attorney, county attorney, or assistant county attorney, as a supervision officer as defined by Section 2, Article 42.12, Code of Criminal Procedure, or as a juvenile probation officer may establish handgun proficiency for the purposes of this subchapter by obtaining from a handgun proficiency instructor approved by the Texas Commission on Law Enforcement for purposes of Section 1702.1675, Occupations Code, a sworn statement that indicates that the person, during the 12-month period preceding the date of the person's application to the department, demonstrated to the instructor proficiency in the use of handguns.

(b) The director by rule shall adopt a procedure by which a person described under Subsection (a) may submit a form demonstrating the person's qualification for an exemption under that subsection. The form must provide sufficient information to allow the department to verify whether the person qualifies for the exemption.

(c) A license issued under this section automatically expires on the six-month anniversary of the date the person's status under Subsection (a) becomes inapplicable. A license that expires under this subsection may be renewed under Section 411.185.

Added by Acts 2007, 80ᵗʰ Leg., R.S., Ch. 1222 (H.B. 2300), Sec. 3, eff. June 15, 2007.
Amended by:
Acts 2009, 81ˢᵗ Leg., R.S., Ch. 1146 (H.B. 2730), Sec. 11.14, eff. Sept. 1, 2009.
Acts 2013, 83ʳᵈ Leg., R.S., Ch. 93 (S.B. 686), Sec. 2.24, eff. May 18, 2013.
Acts 2013, 83ʳᵈ Leg., R.S., Ch. 1302 (H.B. 3142), Sec. 9, eff. June 14, 2013.
Acts 2015, 84ᵗʰ Leg., R.S., Ch. 1029 (H.B. 1376), Sec. 1, eff. Sept. 1, 2015.

GC §411.190. QUALIFIED HANDGUN INSTRUCTORS.

(a) The director may certify as a qualified handgun instructor a person who:

(1) is certified by the Texas Commission on Law Enforcement or under Chapter 1702, Occupations Code, to instruct others in the use of handguns;

(2) regularly instructs others in the use of handguns and has graduated from a handgun instructor school that uses a nationally accepted course designed to

train persons as handgun instructors; or

(3) is certified by the National Rifle Association of America as a handgun instructor.

Text of subsection effective on Jan. 1, 2016

(b) In addition to the qualifications described by Subsection (a), a qualified handgun instructor must be qualified to instruct persons in:

(1) the laws that relate to weapons and to the use of deadly force;

(2) handgun use, proficiency, and safety, including use of restraint holsters and methods to ensure the secure carrying of openly carried handguns;

(3) nonviolent dispute resolution; and

(4) proper storage practices for handguns, including storage practices that eliminate the possibility of accidental injury to a child.

Text of subsection effective on Jan. 1, 2016

(c) In the manner applicable to a person who applies for a license to carry a handgun, the department shall conduct a background check of a person who applies for certification as a qualified handgun instructor. If the background check indicates that the applicant for certification would not qualify to receive a handgun license, the department may not certify the applicant as a qualified handgun instructor. If the background check indicates that the applicant for certification would qualify to receive a handgun license, the department shall provide handgun instructor training to the applicant. The applicant shall pay a fee of $100 to the department for the training. The applicant must take and successfully complete the training offered by the department and pay the training fee before the department may certify the applicant as a qualified handgun instructor. The department shall issue a license to carry a handgun under the authority of this subchapter to any person who is certified as a qualified handgun instructor and who pays to the department a fee of $100 in addition to the training fee. The department by rule may prorate or waive the training fee for an employee of another governmental entity.

(d) The certification of a qualified handgun instructor expires on the second anniversary after the date of certification. To renew a certification, the qualified handgun instructor must pay a fee of $100 and take and successfully complete the retraining courses required by department rule.

(d-1) The department shall ensure that an applicant may renew certification under Subsection (d) from any county in this state by using an online format to complete the required retraining courses if:

(1) the applicant is renewing certification for the first time; or

(2) the applicant completed the required retraining courses in person the previous time the applicant renewed certification.

(e) After certification, a qualified handgun instructor may conduct training for applicants for a license under this subchapter.

Text of subsection effective on Jan. 1, 2016

(f) If the department determines that a reason exists to revoke, suspend, or deny a license to carry a handgun with respect to a person who is a qualified handgun instructor or an applicant for certification as a qualified handgun instructor, the department shall take that action against the person's:

(1) license to carry a handgun if the person is an applicant for or the holder of a license issued under this subchapter; and

(2) certification as a qualified handgun instructor.

Added by Acts 1997, 75th Leg., ch. 165, Sec. 10.01(a), eff. Sept. 1, 1997. Amended by Acts 1999, 76th Leg., ch. 62, Sec. 9.13(a), eff. Sept. 1, 1999; Acts 1999, 76th Leg., ch. 199, Sec. 1, eff. Sept. 1, 1999; Acts 2001, 77th Leg., ch. 1420, Sec. 14.758, eff. Sept. 1, 2001.
Amended by:
Acts 2009, 81st Leg., R.S., Ch. 1146 (H.B. 2730), Sec. 5.11, eff. Sept. 1, 2009.
Acts 2009, 81st Leg., R.S., Ch. 1146 (H.B. 2730), Sec. 11.15, eff. Sept. 1, 2009.
Acts 2011, 82nd Leg., R.S., Ch. 91 (S.B. 1303), Sec. 11.007, eff. Sept. 1, 2011.
Acts 2013, 83rd Leg., R.S., Ch. 93 (S.B. 686), Sec. 2.25, eff. May 18, 2013.
Acts 2015, 84th Leg., R.S., Ch. 437 (H.B. 910), Sec. 23, eff. Jan. 1, 2016.

GC §411.1901. SCHOOL SAFETY CERTIFICATION FOR QUALIFIED HANDGUN INSTRUCTORS.

(a) The department shall establish a process to enable qualified handgun instructors certified under Section 411.190 to obtain an additional certification in school safety. The process must include a school safety certification course that provides training in the following:

(1) the protection of students;

(2) interaction of license holders with first responders;

(3) tactics for denying an intruder entry into a classroom or school facility; and

(4) methods for increasing a license holder's accuracy with a handgun while under duress.

(b) The school safety certification course under Subsection (a) must include not less than 15 hours and not more than 20 hours of instruction.

Text of subsection effective on Jan. 1, 2016

(c) A qualified handgun instructor certified in school safety under this section may provide school safety training, including instruction in the subjects listed under Subsection (a), to employees of a school district or an open-enrollment charter school who hold a license to carry a handgun issued under this subchapter.

(d) The department shall establish a fee in an amount that is sufficient to cover the costs of the school safety certification under this section.

(e) The department may adopt rules to administer this section.

Added by Acts 2013, 83rd Leg., R.S., Ch. 498 (S.B. 1857), Sec. 1, eff. Sept. 1, 2013.
Amended by:
Acts 2015, 84th Leg., R.S., Ch. 437 (H.B. 910), Sec. 24, eff. Jan. 1, 2016.

GC §411.191. REVIEW OF DENIAL, REVOCATION, OR SUSPENSION OF CERTIFICATION AS QUALIFIED HANDGUN INSTRUCTOR.

The procedures for the review of a denial, revocation, or suspension of a license under Section 411.180 apply to the review of a denial, revocation, or suspension of certification as a qualified handgun instructor. The notice provisions of this subchapter relating to denial, revocation, or suspension of handgun licenses apply to the proposed denial, revocation, or suspension of a certification of a qualified handgun instructor or an applicant for certification as a qualified handgun instructor.

Added by Acts 1997, 75th Leg., ch. 165, Sec. 10.01(a), eff. Sept. 1, 1997.

GC §411.192. CONFIDENTIALITY OF RECORDS.

(a) The department shall disclose to a criminal justice agency information contained in its files and records regarding whether a named individual or any individual named in a specified list is licensed under this subchapter. Information on an individual subject to disclosure under this section includes the individual's name, date of birth, gender, race, zip code, telephone number, e-mail address, and Internet website address. Except as otherwise provided by this section and by Section 411.193, all other records maintained under this subchapter are confidential and are not subject to mandatory disclosure under the open records law, Chapter 552.

(b) An applicant or license holder may be furnished a copy of disclosable records regarding the applicant or license holder on request and the payment of a reasonable fee.

(c) The department shall notify a license holder of any request that is made for information relating to the license holder under this section and provide the name of the agency making the request.

(d) The department shall make public and distribute to the public at no cost lists of individuals who are certified as qualified handgun instructors by the department and who request to be included as provided by Subsection (e). The department shall include on the lists each individual's name, telephone number, e-mail address, and Internet website address. The department shall make the list available on the department's Internet website.

(e) An individual who is certified as a qualified handgun instructor may request in writing that the department disclose all or part of the information described by Subsection (d) regarding the individual. The department shall include all or part of the individual's information on the list as requested.

Last amended by Acts 2009, 81ˢᵗ Leg., R.S., Ch. 1146 (H.B. 2730), Sec. 6.03, eff. Sept. 1, 2009.

GC §411.193. STATISTICAL REPORT.

The department shall make available, on request and payment of a reasonable fee to cover costs of copying, a statistical report that includes the number of licenses issued, denied, revoked, or suspended by the department during the preceding month, listed by age, gender, race, and zip code of the applicant or license holder.

Added by Acts 1997, 75ᵗʰ Leg., ch. 165, Sec. 10.01(a), eff. Sept. 1, 1997.

GC §411.194. REDUCTION OF FEES DUE TO INDIGENCY.

(a) Notwithstanding any other provision of this subchapter, the department shall reduce by 50 percent any fee required for the issuance of an original, duplicate, modified, or renewed license under this subchapter if the department determines that the applicant is indigent.

(b) The department shall require an applicant requesting a reduction of a fee to submit proof of indigency with the application materials.

(c) For purposes of this section, an applicant is indigent if the applicant's income is not more than 100 percent of the applicable income level established by the federal poverty guidelines.

Added by Acts 1997, 75ᵗʰ Leg., ch. 165, Sec. 10.01(a), eff. Sept. 1, 1997.

GC §411.195. REDUCTION OF FEES FOR SENIOR CITIZENS. Notwithstanding any other provision of this subchapter, the department shall reduce by 50 percent any fee required for the issuance of an original, duplicate, modified, or renewed license under this subchapter if the applicant for the license is 60 years of age or older.

Last amended by Acts 2005, 79th Leg., Ch. 289 (H.B. 1038), Sec. 1, eff. Sept. 1, 2005.

GC §411.1951. WAIVER OR REDUCTION OF FEES FOR MEMBERS OR VETERANS OF UNITED STATES ARMED FORCES.

(a) In this section, "veteran" means a person who:
  (1) has served in:
    (A) the army, navy, air force, coast guard, or marine corps of the United States;
    (B) the Texas military forces as defined by Section 437.001; or
    (C) an auxiliary service of one of those branches of the armed forces; and
  (2) has been honorably discharged from the branch of the service in which the person served.

(b) Notwithstanding any other provision of this subchapter, the department shall waive any fee required for the issuance of an original, duplicate, modified, or renewed license under this subchapter if the applicant for the license is:
  (1) a member of the United States armed forces, including a member of the reserves, national guard, or state guard; or
  (2) a veteran who, within 365 days preceding the date of the application, was honorably discharged from the branch of service in which the person served.

(c) Notwithstanding any other provision of this subchapter, if the applicant is a veteran who, more than 365 days preceding the date of the application, was honorably discharged from the branch of the service in which the applicant served:
  (1) the applicant must pay a fee of $25 for the issuance of an original or renewed license under this subchapter; and
  (2) the department shall reduce by 50 percent any fee required of the applicant for a duplicate or modified license under this subchapter.

Last amended by Acts 2013, 83rd Leg., R.S., Ch. 1217 (S.B. 1536), Sec. 3.05, eff. Sept. 1, 2013.

GC §411.1952. REDUCTION OF FEES FOR EMPLOYEES OF TEXAS DEPARTMENT OF CRIMINAL JUSTICE. Notwithstanding any other provision of this subchapter, an applicant who is a correctional officer of the Texas Department of Criminal Justice shall pay a fee of $25 for the issuance of an original or renewed license under this subchapter.

Added by Acts 2013, 83rd Leg., R.S., Ch. 251 (H.B. 485), Sec. 2, eff. Sept. 1, 2013.

GC §411.196. METHOD OF PAYMENT. A person may pay a fee required by this subchapter by cash, credit card, personal check, cashier's check, or money order. A person who pays a fee required by this subchapter by cash must pay the fee in person. Checks or money orders must be made payable to the "Texas Department of Public Safety." A person whose payment for a fee required by this subchapter is dishonored or reversed must pay any future fees required by this subchapter by cashier's check or money order made payable to the "Texas

Department of Public Safety." A fee received by the department under this subchapter is nonrefundable.

Last amended by Acts 2005, 79th Leg., Ch. 1065 (H.B. 1483), Sec. 1, eff. Sept. 1, 2005.

GC §411.197. RULES. The director shall adopt rules to administer this subchapter.

Added by Acts 1997, 75th Leg., ch. 165, Sec. 10.01(a), eff. Sept. 1, 1997.

GC §411.198. LAW ENFORCEMENT OFFICER ALIAS HANDGUN LICENSE.

Text of subsection effective on Jan. 1, 2016

(a) On written approval of the director, the department may issue to a law enforcement officer an alias license to carry a handgun to be used in supervised activities involving criminal investigations.

(b) It is a defense to prosecution under Section 46.035, Penal Code, that the actor, at the time of the commission of the offense, was the holder of an alias license issued under this section.

Added by Acts 1997, 75th Leg., ch. 165, Sec. 10.01(a), eff. Sept. 1, 1997.
Amended by:
Acts 2015, 84th Leg., R.S., Ch. 437 (H.B. 910), Sec. 25, eff. Jan. 1, 2016.

GC §411.199. HONORABLY RETIRED PEACE OFFICERS.

(a) A person who is licensed as a peace officer under Chapter 1701, Occupations Code, and who has been employed full-time as a peace officer by a law enforcement agency may apply for a license under this subchapter at any time after retirement.

(b) The person shall submit two complete sets of legible and classifiable fingerprints and a sworn statement from the head of the law enforcement agency employing the applicant. A head of a law enforcement agency may not refuse to issue a statement under this subsection. If the applicant alleges that the statement is untrue, the department shall investigate the validity of the statement. The statement must include:

(1) the name and rank of the applicant;

(2) the status of the applicant before retirement;

(3) whether or not the applicant was accused of misconduct at the time of the retirement;

(4) the physical and mental condition of the applicant;

(5) the type of weapons the applicant had demonstrated proficiency with during the last year of employment;

(6) whether the applicant would be eligible for reemployment with the agency, and if not, the reasons the applicant is not eligible; and

(7) a recommendation from the agency head regarding the issuance of a license under this subchapter.

(c) The department may issue a license under this subchapter to an applicant under this section if the applicant is honorably retired and physically and emotionally fit to possess a handgun. In this subsection, "honorably retired" means the applicant:

(1) did not retire in lieu of any disciplinary action;

(2) was eligible to retire from the law enforcement agency or was ineligible to retire only as a result of an injury received in the course of the applicant's employment with the agency; and

(3) is entitled to receive a pension or annuity for service as a law enforcement officer or is not entitled to receive a pension or annuity only because the law enforcement agency that employed the applicant does not offer a pension or annuity to its employees.

(d) An applicant under this section must pay a fee of $25 for a license issued under this subchapter.

(e) *Repealed by Acts 2015, 84th Leg., R.S., Ch. 1236 , Sec. 9.007, eff. Sept. 1, 2015.*

(f) A license issued under this section expires as provided by Section 411.183.

(g) A retired officer of the United States who was eligible to carry a firearm in the discharge of the officer's official duties is eligible for a license under this section. An applicant described by this subsection may submit the application at any time after retirement. The applicant shall submit with the application proper proof of retired status by presenting the following documents prepared by the agency from which the applicant retired:

(1) retirement credentials; and

(2) a letter from the agency head stating the applicant retired in good standing.

Added by Acts 1997, 75th Leg., ch. 165, Sec. 10.01(a), eff. Sept. 1, 1997. Amended by Acts 1999, 76th Leg., ch. 25, Sec. 1, eff. May 3, 1999; Acts 1999, 76th Leg., ch. 62, Sec. 9.14, eff. Sept. 1, 1999; Acts 2001, 77th Leg., ch. 196, Sec. 1, eff. Sept. 1, 2001.
Amended by:
Acts 2009, 81st Leg., R.S., Ch. 1146 (H.B. 2730), Sec. 11.16, eff. Sept. 1, 2009.
Acts 2013, 83rd Leg., R.S., Ch. 1302 (H.B. 3142), Sec. 10, eff. June 14, 2013.
Acts 2013, 83rd Leg., R.S., Ch. 1387 (H.B. 48), Sec. 5, eff. Sept. 1, 2013.
Acts 2015, 84th Leg., R.S., Ch. 1236 (S.B. 1296), Sec. 9.007, eff. Sept. 1, 2015.

GC §411.1991. PEACE OFFICERS.

(a) A person who is licensed as a peace officer under Chapter 1701, Occupations Code, and employed as a peace officer by a law enforcement agency, or who is a member of the Texas military forces, excluding Texas State Guard members who are serving in the Texas Legislature, may apply for a license under this subchapter.

(a-1) An applicant who is a peace officer shall submit to the department:

(1) the name and rank of the applicant; and

(2) a current copy of the applicant's peace officer license and evidence of employment as a peace officer.

(a-2) The department shall adopt rules regarding the information required to be included in an application submitted by a member of the Texas military forces under this section.

(b) The department may issue a license under this subchapter to an applicant under this section if the applicant complies with Subsection (a-1) or rules adopted under Subsection (a-2), as applicable.

(c) An applicant under this section shall pay a fee of $25 for a license issued under this subchapter.

(d) A license issued under this section expires as provided by Section 411.183.

Added by Acts 1999, 76th Leg., ch. 62, Sec. 9.15(a), eff. Sept. 1, 1999.
Amended by:
Acts 2009, 81st Leg., R.S., Ch. 1146 (H.B. 2730), Sec. 11.17, eff. Sept. 1, 2009.

Acts 2013, 83ʳᵈ Leg., R.S., Ch. 251 (H.B. 485), Sec. 3, eff. Sept. 1, 2013.
Acts 2013, 83ʳᵈ Leg., R.S., Ch. 251 (H.B. 485), Sec. 4, eff. Sept. 1, 2013.
Acts 2015, 84ᵗʰ Leg., R.S., Ch. 174 (H.B. 2604), Sec. 1, eff. Sept. 1, 2015.

GC §411.1992. FORMER RESERVE LAW ENFORCEMENT OFFICERS.

(a) A person who served as a reserve law enforcement officer, as defined by Section 1701.001, Occupations Code, not less than a total of 15 years with one or more state or local law enforcement agencies may apply for a license under this subchapter at any time.

(b) The applicant shall submit to the department two complete sets of legible and classifiable fingerprints and a sworn statement from the head of the law enforcement agency at which the applicant last served as a reserve law enforcement officer. A head of a law enforcement agency may not refuse to issue a statement under this subsection. If the applicant alleges that the statement is untrue, the department shall investigate the validity of the statement. The statement must include:

  (1) the name and rank of the applicant;
  (2) the status of the applicant;
  (3) whether the applicant was accused of misconduct at any time during the applicant's term of service and the disposition of that accusation;
  (4) a description of the physical and mental condition of the applicant;
  (5) a list of the types of weapons the applicant demonstrated proficiency with during the applicant's term of service; and
  (6) a recommendation from the agency head regarding the issuance of a license under this subchapter.

(c) The department may issue a license under this subchapter to an applicant under this section if the applicant was a reserve law enforcement officer for not less than a total of 15 years with one or more state or local law enforcement agencies and is physically and emotionally fit to possess a handgun.

(d) An applicant under this section must pay a fee of $25 for a license issued under this subchapter.

(e) A former reserve law enforcement officer who obtains a license as provided by this section must maintain, for the category of weapon licensed, the proficiency required for the person under Section 1701.357, Occupations Code. The department or the local law enforcement agency at which the person last served as a reserve law enforcement officer shall allow the person an opportunity to annually demonstrate the required proficiency. The proficiency shall be reported to the department on application and renewal.

(f) A license issued under this section expires as provided by Section 411.183.

Added by Acts 2013, 83ʳᵈ Leg., R.S., Ch. 1080 (H.B. 3370), Sec. 1, eff. Sept. 1, 2013.

GC §411.200. APPLICATION TO LICENSED SECURITY OFFICERS. This
subchapter does not exempt a license holder who is also employed as a security officer and licensed under Chapter 1702, Occupations Code, from the duty to comply with Chapter 1702, Occupations Code, or Section 46.02, Penal Code.

Last amended by Acts 2001, 77ᵗʰ Leg., ch. 1420, Sec. 14.759, eff. Sept. 1, 2001.

GC §411.201. ACTIVE AND RETIRED JUDICIAL OFFICERS.

(a) In this section:
  (1) "Active judicial officer" means:

(A) a person serving as a judge or justice of the supreme court, the court of criminal appeals, a court of appeals, a district court, a criminal district court, a constitutional county court, a statutory county court, a justice court, or a municipal court;

(B) a federal judge who is a resident of this state; or

(C) a person appointed and serving as an associate judge under Chapter 201, Family Code.

(2) "Federal judge" means:

(A) a judge of a United States court of appeals;

(B) a judge of a United States district court;

(C) a judge of a United States bankruptcy court; or

(D) a magistrate judge of a United States district court.

(3) "Retired judicial officer" means:

(A) a visiting judge appointed under Section 26.023 or 26.024;

(B) a senior judge designated under Section 75.001 or a judicial officer as designated or defined by Section 75.001, 831.001, or 836.001; or

(C) a retired federal judge who is a resident of this state.

(b) Notwithstanding any other provision of this subchapter, the department shall issue a license under this subchapter to an active or retired judicial officer who meets the requirements of this section.

Text of subsection effective on Jan. 1, 2016

(c) An active judicial officer is eligible for a license to carry a handgun under the authority of this subchapter. A retired judicial officer is eligible for a license to carry a handgun under the authority of this subchapter if the officer:

(1) has not been convicted of a felony;

(2) has not, in the five years preceding the date of application, been convicted of a Class A or Class B misdemeanor or equivalent offense;

(3) is not charged with the commission of a Class A or Class B misdemeanor or equivalent offense or of a felony under an information or indictment;

(4) is not a chemically dependent person; and

(5) is not a person of unsound mind.

Text of subsection effective on Jan. 1, 2016

(d) An applicant for a license who is an active or retired judicial officer must submit to the department:

(1) a completed application, including all required affidavits, on a form prescribed by the department;

(2) one or more photographs of the applicant that meet the requirements of the department;

(3) two complete sets of legible and classifiable fingerprints of the applicant, including one set taken by a person employed by a law enforcement agency who is appropriately trained in recording fingerprints;

(4) evidence of handgun proficiency, in the form and manner required by the department for an applicant under this section;

(5) a nonrefundable application and license fee set by the department in an amount reasonably designed to cover the administrative costs associated with issuance of a license to carry a handgun under this subchapter; and

(6) if the applicant is a retired judicial officer, a form executed by the applicant that authorizes the department to make an inquiry into any noncriminal history

records that are necessary to determine the applicant's eligibility for a license under this subchapter.

Text of subsection effective on Jan. 1, 2016

(e) On receipt of all the application materials required by this section, the department shall:
    (1) if the applicant is an active judicial officer, issue a license to carry a handgun under the authority of this subchapter; or
    (2) if the applicant is a retired judicial officer, conduct an appropriate background investigation to determine the applicant's eligibility for the license and, if the applicant is eligible, issue a license to carry a handgun under the authority of this subchapter.
(f) Except as otherwise provided by this subsection, an applicant for a license under this section must satisfy the handgun proficiency requirements of Section 411.188. The classroom instruction part of the proficiency course for an active judicial officer is not subject to a minimum hour requirement. The instruction must include instruction only on:
    (1) handgun use, proficiency, and safety; and
    (2) proper storage practices for handguns with an emphasis on storage practices that eliminate the possibility of accidental injury to a child.
(g) A license issued under this section expires as provided by Section 411.183 and may be renewed in accordance with Section 411.185.

Text of subsection effective on Jan. 1, 2016

(h) The department shall issue a license to carry a handgun under the authority of this subchapter to an elected attorney representing the state in the prosecution of felony cases who meets the requirements of this section for an active judicial officer. The department shall waive any fee required for the issuance of an original, duplicate, or renewed license under this subchapter for an applicant who is an attorney elected or employed to represent the state in the prosecution of felony cases.

Added by Acts 1997, 75th Leg., ch. 165, Sec. 10.01(a), eff. Sept. 1, 1997.
Amended by:
Acts 2007, 80th Leg., R.S., Ch. 402 (S.B. 835), Sec. 1, eff. June 15, 2007.
Acts 2007, 80th Leg., R.S., Ch. 1222 (H.B. 2300), Sec. 4, eff. June 15, 2007.
Acts 2009, 81st Leg., R.S., Ch. 1146 (H.B. 2730), Sec. 11.18, eff. Sept. 1, 2009.
Acts 2011, 82nd Leg., 1st C.S., Ch. 3 (H.B. 79), Sec. 13.01, eff. Sept. 28, 2011.
Acts 2013, 83rd Leg., R.S., Ch. 1387 (H.B. 48), Sec. 4, eff. Sept. 1, 2013.
Acts 2015, 84th Leg., R.S., Ch. 437 (H.B. 910), Sec. 26, eff. Jan. 1, 2016.
Acts 2015, 84th Leg., R.S., Ch. 587 (H.B. 3747), Sec. 1, eff. June 16, 2015.

GC §411.202. LICENSE A BENEFIT. The issuance of a license under this subchapter is a benefit to the license holder for purposes of those sections of the Penal Code to which the definition of "benefit" under Section 1.07, Penal Code, applies.

Added by Acts 1997, 75th Leg., ch. 165, Sec. 10.01(a), eff. Sept. 1, 1997.

GC §411.203. RIGHTS OF EMPLOYERS. This subchapter does not prevent or otherwise limit the right of a public or private employer to prohibit persons who are licensed under this subchapter from carrying a concealed handgun on the premises of the business. In this section, "premises" has the meaning assigned by Section 46.035(f)(3), Penal Code.

Added by Acts 1997, 75ᵗʰ Leg., ch. 165, Sec. 10.01(a), eff. Sept. 1, 1997.
Amended by:
Acts 2011, 82ⁿᵈ Leg., R.S., Ch. 1058 (S.B. 321), Sec. 2, eff. Sept. 1, 2011.
Acts 2015, 84ᵗʰ Leg., R.S., Ch. 437 (H.B. 910), Sec. 27, eff. Jan. 1, 2016.

GC §411.2031. CARRYING OF HANDGUNS BY LICENSE HOLDERS ON CERTAIN CAMPUSES.

(a) For purposes of this section:

(1) "Campus" means all land and buildings owned or leased by an institution of higher education or private or independent institution of higher education.

(2) "Institution of higher education" and "private or independent institution of higher education" have the meanings assigned by Section 61.003, Education Code.

(3) "Premises" has the meaning assigned by Section 46.035, Penal Code.

(b) A license holder may carry a concealed handgun on or about the license holder's person while the license holder is on the campus of an institution of higher education or private or independent institution of higher education in this state.

(c) Except as provided by Subsection (d), (d-1), or (e), an institution of higher education or private or independent institution of higher education in this state may not adopt any rule, regulation, or other provision prohibiting license holders from carrying handguns on the campus of the institution.

(d) An institution of higher education or private or independent institution of higher education in this state may establish rules, regulations, or other provisions concerning the storage of handguns in dormitories or other residential facilities that are owned or leased and operated by the institution and located on the campus of the institution.

(d-1) After consulting with students, staff, and faculty of the institution regarding the nature of the student population, specific safety considerations, and the uniqueness of the campus environment, the president or other chief executive officer of an institution of higher education in this state shall establish reasonable rules, regulations, or other provisions regarding the carrying of concealed handguns by license holders on the campus of the institution or on premises located on the campus of the institution. The president or officer may not establish provisions that generally prohibit or have the effect of generally prohibiting license holders from carrying concealed handguns on the campus of the institution. The president or officer may amend the provisions as necessary for campus safety. The provisions take effect as determined by the president or officer unless subsequently amended by the board of regents or other governing board under Subsection (d-2). The institution must give effective notice under Section 30.06, Penal Code, with respect to any portion of a premises on which license holders may not carry.

(d-2) Not later than the 90th day after the date that the rules, regulations, or other provisions are established as described by Subsection (d-1), the board of regents or other governing board of the institution of higher education shall review the provisions. The board of regents or other governing board may, by a vote of not less than two-thirds of the board, amend wholly or partly the provisions established under Subsection (d-1). If amended under this subsection, the provisions are considered to be those of the institution as established under Subsection (d-1).

(d-3) An institution of higher education shall widely distribute the rules, regulations, or other provisions described by Subsection (d-1) to the institution's students, staff, and faculty, including by prominently publishing the provisions on the institution's Internet website.

(d-4) Not later than Sept. 1 of each even-numbered year, each institution of higher education in this state shall submit a report to the legislature and to the standing committees of the legislature with jurisdiction over the implementation and continuation of this section that:

(1) describes its rules, regulations, or other provisions regarding the carrying of concealed handguns on the campus of the institution; and

(2) explains the reasons the institution has established those provisions.

(e) A private or independent institution of higher education in this state, after consulting with students, staff, and faculty of the institution, may establish rules, regulations, or other provisions prohibiting license holders from carrying handguns on the campus of the institution, any grounds or building on which an activity sponsored by the institution is being conducted, or a passenger transportation vehicle owned by the institution.

Added by Acts 2015, 84'h Leg., R.S., Ch. 438 (S.B. 11), Sec. 1, eff. Aug. 1, 2016.

GC §411.2032. TRANSPORTATION AND STORAGE OF FIREARMS AND AMMUNITION BY LICENSE HOLDERS IN PRIVATE VEHICLES ON CERTAIN CAMPUSES.

(a) For purposes of this section:

(1) "Campus" means all land and buildings owned or leased by an institution of higher education or private or independent institution of higher education.

(2) "Institution of higher education" and "private or independent institution of higher education" have the meanings assigned by Section 61.003, Education Code.

Text of subsection effective on Jan. 1, 2016

(b) An institution of higher education or private or independent institution of higher education in this state may not adopt or enforce any rule, regulation, or other provision or take any other action, including posting notice under Section 30.06 or 30.07, Penal Code, prohibiting or placing restrictions on the storage or transportation of a firearm or ammunition in a locked, privately owned or leased motor vehicle by a person, including a student enrolled at that institution, who holds a license to carry a handgun under this subchapter and lawfully possesses the firearm or ammunition:

(1) on a street or driveway located on the campus of the institution; or

(2) in a parking lot, parking garage, or other parking area located on the campus of the institution.

Added by Acts 2013, 83rd Leg., R.S., Ch. 1248 (S.B. 1907), Sec. 1, eff. Sept. 1, 2013. Amended by:
Acts 2015, 84th Leg., R.S., Ch. 437 (H.B. 910), Sec. 28, eff. Jan. 1, 2016.

GC §411.204. NOTICE REQUIRED ON CERTAIN PREMISES. (a) A business that has a permit or license issued under Chapter 25, 28, 32, 69, or 74, Alcoholic

Beverage Code, and that derives 51 percent or more of its income from the sale of alcoholic beverages for on-premises consumption as determined by the Texas Alcoholic Beverage Commission under Section 104.06, Alcoholic Beverage Code, shall prominently display at each entrance to the business premises a sign that complies with the requirements of Subsection (c).

(b) A hospital licensed under Chapter 241, Health and Safety Code, or a nursing home licensed under Chapter 242, Health and Safety Code, shall prominently display at each entrance to the hospital or nursing home, as appropriate, a sign that complies with the requirements of Subsection (c) other than the requirement that the sign include on its face the number "51".

(c) The sign required under Subsections (a) and (b) must give notice in both English and Spanish that it is unlawful for a person licensed under this subchapter to carry a handgun on the premises. The sign must appear in contrasting colors with block letters at least one inch in height and must include on its face the number "51" printed in solid red at least five inches in height. The sign shall be displayed in a conspicuous manner clearly visible to the public.

(d) A business that has a permit or license issued under the Alcoholic Beverage Code and that is not required to display a sign under this section may be required to display a sign under Section 11.041 or 61.11, Alcoholic Beverage Code.

(e) This section does not apply to a business that has a food and beverage certificate issued under the Alcoholic Beverage Code.

Last amended by Acts 1999, 76th Leg., ch. 62, Sec. 9.16(a), eff. Sept. 1, 1999; Acts 1999, 76th Leg., ch. 523, Sec. 1, eff. June 18, 1999.

GC §411.205. REQUIREMENT TO DISPLAY LICENSE.

If a license holder is carrying a handgun on or about the license holder's person when a magistrate or a peace officer demands that the license holder display identification, the license holder shall display both the license holder's driver's license or identification certificate issued by the department and the license holder's handgun license.

Last amended by Acts 2009, 81st Leg., R.S., Ch. 1146 (H.B. 2730), Sec. 12A.02, eff. Sept. 1, 2009.

GC §411.206. SEIZURE OF HANDGUN AND LICENSE.

(a) If a peace officer arrests and takes into custody a license holder who is carrying a handgun under the authority of this subchapter, the officer shall seize the license holder's handgun and license as evidence.

(b) The provisions of Article 18.19, Code of Criminal Procedure, relating to the disposition of weapons seized in connection with criminal offenses, apply to a handgun seized under this subsection.

(c) Any judgment of conviction entered by any court for an offense under Section 46.035, Penal Code, must contain the handgun license number of the convicted license holder. A certified copy of the judgment is conclusive and sufficient evidence to justify revocation of a license under Section 411.186(a)(4).

Added by Acts 1997, 75th Leg., ch. 165, Sec. 10.01(a), eff. Sept. 1, 1997.

GC §411.207. AUTHORITY OF PEACE OFFICER TO DISARM.

(a) A peace officer who is acting in the lawful discharge of the officer's official duties may disarm a license holder at any time the officer reasonably believes it is necessary for the protection of the license holder, officer, or another individual. The peace officer shall return the handgun to the license holder before discharging the license holder from the scene if the officer determines that the license holder is not a threat to the officer, license holder, or another individual and if the license holder has not violated any provision of this subchapter or committed any other violation that results in the arrest of the license holder.

(b) A peace officer who is acting in the lawful discharge of the officer's official duties may temporarily disarm a license holder when a license holder enters a non-public, secure portion of a law enforcement facility, if the law enforcement agency provides a gun locker where the peace officer can secure the license holder's handgun. The peace officer shall secure the handgun in the locker and shall return the handgun to the license holder immediately after the license holder leaves the non-public, secure portion of the law enforcement facility.

(c) A law enforcement facility shall prominently display at each entrance to a non-public, secure portion of the facility a sign that gives notice in both English and Spanish that, under this section, a peace officer may temporarily disarm a license holder when the license holder enters the non-public, secure portion of the facility. The sign must appear in contrasting colors with block letters at least one inch in height. The sign shall be displayed in a clearly visible and conspicuous manner.

(d) In this section:

   (1) "Law enforcement facility" means a building or a portion of a building used exclusively by a law enforcement agency that employs peace officers as described by Articles 2.12(1) and (3), Code of Criminal Procedure, and support personnel to conduct the official business of the agency. The term does not include:

      (A) any portion of a building not actively used exclusively to conduct the official business of the agency; or

      (B) any public or private driveway, street, sidewalk, walkway, parking lot, parking garage, or other parking area.

   (2) "Non-public, secure portion of a law enforcement facility" means that portion of a law enforcement facility to which the general public is denied access without express permission and to which access is granted solely to conduct the official business of the law enforcement agency.

Last amended by Acts 2007, 80th Leg., R.S., Ch. 572 (S.B. 1709), Sec. 1, eff. Sept. 1, 2007.

GC §411.208. LIMITATION OF LIABILITY.

Text of subsection effective on Aug. 1, 2016

(a) A court may not hold the state, an agency or subdivision of the state, an officer or employee of the state, an institution of higher education, an officer or employee of an institution of higher education, a private or independent institution of higher education that has not adopted rules under Section 411.2031(e), an officer or employee of a private or independent institution of higher education that has not adopted rules under Section 411.2031(e), a peace officer, or a qualified handgun instructor liable for damages caused by:

   (1) an action authorized under this subchapter or a failure to perform a duty imposed by this subchapter; or

   (2) the actions of an applicant or license holder that occur after the applicant has received a license or been denied a license under this subchapter.

Text of subsection effective until Aug. 1, 2016

(b) A cause of action in damages may not be brought against the state, an agency or subdivision of the state, an officer or employee of the state, a peace officer, or a qualified handgun instructor for any damage caused by the actions of an applicant or license holder under this subchapter.

Text of subsection effective on Aug. 1, 2016

(b) A cause of action in damages may not be brought against the state, an agency or subdivision of the state, an officer or employee of the state, an institution of higher education, an officer or employee of an institution of higher education, a private or independent institution of higher education that has not adopted rules under Section 411.2031(e), an officer or employee of a private or independent institution of higher education that has not adopted rules under Section 411.2031(e), a peace officer, or a qualified handgun instructor for any damage caused by the actions of an applicant or license holder under this subchapter.
(c) The department is not responsible for any injury or damage inflicted on any person by an applicant or license holder arising or alleged to have arisen from an action taken by the department under this subchapter.

Text of subsection effective until Aug. 1, 2016

(d) The immunities granted under Subsections (a), (b), and (c) do not apply to an act or a failure to act by the state, an agency or subdivision of the state, an officer of the state, or a peace officer if the act or failure to act was capricious or arbitrary.

Text of subsection effective on Aug. 1, 2016

(d) The immunities granted under Subsections (a), (b), and (c) do not apply to:
  (1) an act or a failure to act by the state, an agency or subdivision of the state, an officer of the state, an institution of higher education, an officer or employee of an institution of higher education, a private or independent institution of higher education that has not adopted rules under Section 411.2031(e), an officer or employee of a private or independent institution of higher education that has not adopted rules under Section 411.2031(e), or a peace officer if the act or failure to act was capricious or arbitrary; or
  (2) any officer or employee of an institution of higher education or private or independent institution of higher education described by Subdivision (1) who possesses a handgun on the campus of that institution and whose conduct with regard to the handgun is made the basis of a claim for personal injury or property damage.
(e) The immunities granted under Subsection (a) to a qualified handgun instructor do not apply to a cause of action for fraud or a deceptive trade practice.

Text of subsection effective on Aug. 1, 2016

(f) For purposes of this section:
  (1) "Campus" has the meaning assigned by Section 411.2031.
  (2) "Institution of higher education" and "private or independent institution of

higher education" have the meanings assigned by Section 61.003, Education Code.

Added by Acts 1997, 75th Leg., ch. 165, Sec. 10.01(a), eff. Sept. 1, 1997.
Amended by:
Acts 2009, 81st Leg., R.S., Ch. 1146 (H.B. 2730), Sec. 11.19, eff. Sept. 1, 2009.
Acts 2015, 84th Leg., R.S., Ch. 438 (S.B. 11), Sec. 2, eff. Aug. 1, 2016.

GC §411.209. WRONGFUL EXCLUSION OF CONCEALED HANDGUN LICENSE HOLDER.

(a) A state agency or a political subdivision of the state may not provide notice by a communication described by Section 30.06, Penal Code, or by any sign expressly referring to that law or to a concealed handgun license, that a license holder carrying a handgun under the authority of this subchapter is prohibited from entering or remaining on a premises or other place owned or leased by the governmental entity unless license holders are prohibited from carrying a handgun on the premises or other place by Section 46.03 or 46.035, Penal Code.

(b) A state agency or a political subdivision of the state that violates Subsection (a) is liable for a civil penalty of:

(1) not less than $1,000 and not more than $1,500 for the first violation; and

(2) not less than $10,000 and not more than $10,500 for the second or a subsequent violation.

(c) Each day of a continuing violation of Subsection (a) constitutes a separate violation.

(d) A citizen of this state or a person licensed to carry a concealed handgun under this subchapter may file a complaint with the attorney general that a state agency or political subdivision is in violation of Subsection (a) if the citizen or person provides the agency or subdivision a written notice that describes the violation and specific location of the sign found to be in violation and the agency or subdivision does not cure the violation before the end of the third business day after the date of receiving the written notice. A complaint filed under this subsection must include evidence of the violation and a copy of the written notice.

(e) A civil penalty collected by the attorney general under this section shall be deposited to the credit of the compensation to victims of crime fund established under Subchapter B, Chapter 56, Code of Criminal Procedure.

(f) Before a suit may be brought against a state agency or a political subdivision of the state for a violation of Subsection (a), the attorney general must investigate the complaint to determine whether legal action is warranted. If legal action is warranted, the attorney general must give the chief administrative officer of the agency or political subdivision charged with the violation a written notice that:

(1) describes the violation and specific location of the sign found to be in violation;

(2) states the amount of the proposed penalty for the violation; and

(3) gives the agency or political subdivision 15 days from receipt of the notice to remove the sign and cure the violation to avoid the penalty, unless the agency or political subdivision was found liable by a court for previously violating Subsection (a).

(g) If the attorney general determines that legal action is warranted and that the state agency or political subdivision has not cured the violation within the 15-day period provided by Subsection (f)(3), the attorney general or the appropriate county or district attorney may sue to collect the civil penalty provided by Subsection (b). The attorney general may also file a petition for a writ of mandamus or apply for other appropriate equitable relief. A suit or petition under this subsection may be filed in a district court in Travis County or in a county in which the principal office of the state agency or political subdivision is located. The attorney general may recover reasonable expenses incurred in obtaining relief under this subsection, including court costs, reasonable attorney's fees, investigative costs, witness fees, and deposition costs.

(h) Sovereign immunity to suit is waived and abolished to the extent of liability created by this section.

Added by Acts 2015, 84th Leg., R.S., Ch. 593 (S.B. 273), Sec. 1, eff. Sept. 1, 2015.

PENAL CODE

Chapter 9. JUSTIFICATION EXCLUDING CRIMINAL RESPONSIBILITY
Subchapter A GENERAL PROVISIONS

PC §9.01. DEFINITIONS. In this chapter:

(1) "Custody" has the meaning assigned by Section 38.01.

(2) "Escape" has the meaning assigned by Section 38.01.

(3) "Deadly force" means force that is intended or known by the actor to cause, or in the manner of its use or intended use is capable of causing, death or serious bodily injury.

(4) "Habitation" has the meaning assigned by Section 30.01.

(5) "Vehicle" has the meaning assigned by Section 30.01.

Last amended by Acts 2007, 80th Leg., R.S., Ch. 1 (S.B. 378), Sec. 1, eff. Sept. 1, 2007.

PC §9.02. JUSTIFICATION AS A DEFENSE. It is a defense to prosecution that the conduct in question is justified under this chapter.

Last amended by Acts 1993, 73rd Leg., ch. 900, Sec. 1.01, eff. Sept. 1, 1994.

PC §9.03. CONFINEMENT AS JUSTIFIABLE FORCE. Confinement is justified when force is justified by this chapter if the actor takes reasonable measures to terminate the confinement as soon as he knows he safely can unless the person confined has been arrested for an offense.

Last amended by Acts 1993, 73rd Leg., ch. 900, Sec. 1.01, eff. Sept. 1, 1994.

PC §9.04. THREATS AS JUSTIFIABLE FORCE. The threat of force is justified when the use of force is justified by this chapter. For purposes of this section, a threat to cause death or serious bodily injury by the production of a weapon or otherwise, as long as the actor's purpose is limited to creating an apprehension that he will use deadly force if necessary, does not constitute the use of deadly force.

Last amended by Acts 1993, 73rd Leg., ch. 900, Sec. 1.01, eff. Sept. 1, 1994.

PC §9.05. RECKLESS INJURY OF INNOCENT THIRD PERSON. Even though an actor is justified under this chapter in threatening or using force or deadly force against another, if in doing so he also recklessly injures or kills an innocent third person, the justification afforded by this chapter is unavailable in a prosecution for the reckless injury or killing of the innocent third person.

Last amended by Acts 1993, 73ʳᵈ Leg., ch. 900, Sec. 1.01, eff. Sept. 1, 1994.

PC §9.06. CIVIL REMEDIES UNAFFECTED. The fact that conduct is justified under this chapter does not abolish or impair any remedy for the conduct that is available in a civil suit.

Last amended by Acts 1993, 73ʳᵈ Leg., ch. 900, Sec. 1.01, eff. Sept. 1, 1994.

Subchapter B. JUSTIFICATION GENERALLY

PC §9.21. PUBLIC DUTY.
(a) Except as qualified by Subsections (b) and (c), conduct is justified if the actor reasonably believes the conduct is required or authorized by law, by the judgment or order of a competent court or other governmental tribunal, or in the execution of legal process.
(b) The other sections of this chapter control when force is used against a person to protect persons (Subchapter C), to protect property (Subchapter D), for law enforcement (Subchapter E), or by virtue of a special relationship (Subchapter F).
(c) The use of deadly force is not justified under this section unless the actor reasonably believes the deadly force is specifically required by statute or unless it occurs in the lawful conduct of war. If deadly force is so justified, there is no duty to retreat before using it.
(d) The justification afforded by this section is available if the actor reasonably believes:
   (1) the court or governmental tribunal has jurisdiction or the process is lawful, even though the court or governmental tribunal lacks jurisdiction or the process is unlawful; or
   (2) his conduct is required or authorized to assist a public servant in the performance of his official duty, even though the servant exceeds his lawful authority.

Last amended by Acts 1993, 73ʳᵈ Leg., ch. 900, Sec. 1.01, eff. Sept. 1, 1994.

PC §9.22. NECESSITY. Conduct is justified if:
   (1) the actor reasonably believes the conduct is immediately necessary to avoid imminent harm;
   (2) the desirability and urgency of avoiding the harm clearly outweigh, according to ordinary standards of reasonableness, the harm sought to be prevented by the law proscribing the conduct; and
   (3) a legislative purpose to exclude the justification claimed for the conduct does not otherwise plainly appear.

Last amended by Acts 1993, 73ʳᵈ Leg., ch. 900, Sec. 1.01, eff. Sept. 1, 1994.

Subchapter C. PROTECTION OF PERSONS

PC §9.31. SELF-DEFENSE.
(a) Except as provided in Subsection (b), a person is justified in using force against another when and to the degree the actor reasonably believes the force

is immediately necessary to protect the actor against the other's use or attempted use of unlawful force. The actor's belief that the force was immediately necessary as described by this subsection is presumed to be reasonable if the actor:

(1) knew or had reason to believe that the person against whom the force was used:

(A) unlawfully and with force entered, or was attempting to enter unlawfully and with force, the actor's occupied habitation, vehicle, or place of business or employment;

(B) unlawfully and with force removed, or was attempting to remove unlawfully and with force, the actor from the actor's habitation, vehicle, or place of business or employment; or

(C) was committing or attempting to commit aggravated kidnapping, murder, sexual assault, aggravated sexual assault, robbery, or aggravated robbery;

(2) did not provoke the person against whom the force was used; and

(3) was not otherwise engaged in criminal activity, other than a Class C misdemeanor that is a violation of a law or ordinance regulating traffic at the time the force was used.

(b) The use of force against another is not justified:

(1) in response to verbal provocation alone;

(2) to resist an arrest or search that the actor knows is being made by a peace officer, or by a person acting in a peace officer's presence and at his direction, even though the arrest or search is unlawful, unless the resistance is justified under Subsection (c);

(3) if the actor consented to the exact force used or attempted by the other;

(4) if the actor provoked the other's use or attempted use of unlawful force, unless:

(A) the actor abandons the encounter, or clearly communicates to the other his intent to do so reasonably believing he cannot safely abandon the encounter; and

(B) the other nevertheless continues or attempts to use unlawful force against the actor; or

(5) if the actor sought an explanation from or discussion with the other person concerning the actor's differences with the other person while the actor was:

(A) carrying a weapon in violation of Section 46.02; or

(B) possessing or transporting a weapon in violation of Section 46.05.

(c) The use of force to resist an arrest or search is justified:

(1) if, before the actor offers any resistance, the peace officer (or person acting at his direction) uses or attempts to use greater force than necessary to make the arrest or search; and

(2) when and to the degree the actor reasonably believes the force is immediately necessary to protect himself against the peace officer's (or other person's) use or attempted use of greater force than necessary.

(d) The use of deadly force is not justified under this subchapter except as provided in Sections 9.32, 9.33, and 9.34.

(e) A person who has a right to be present at the location where the force is used, who has not provoked the person against whom the force is used, and who is not engaged in criminal activity at the time the force is used is not required to retreat before using force as described by this section.

(f) For purposes of Subsection (a), in determining whether an actor described by Subsection (e) reasonably believed that the use of force was necessary, a finder of fact may not consider whether the actor failed to retreat.

Last amended by Acts 2007, 80th Leg., R.S., Ch. 1 (S.B. 378), Sec. 2, eff. Sept. 1, 2007.

PC §9.32. DEADLY FORCE IN DEFENSE OF PERSON.

(a) A person is justified in using deadly force against another:

(1) if the actor would be justified in using force against the other under Section 9.31; and

(2) when and to the degree the actor reasonably believes the deadly force is immediately necessary:

(A) to protect the actor against the other's use or attempted use of unlawful deadly force; or

(B) to prevent the other's imminent commission of aggravated kidnapping, murder, sexual assault, aggravated sexual assault, robbery, or aggravated robbery.

(b) The actor's belief under Subsection (a)(2) that the deadly force was immediately necessary as described by that subdivision is presumed to be reasonable if the actor:

(1) knew or had reason to believe that the person against whom the deadly force was used:

(A) unlawfully and with force entered, or was attempting to enter unlawfully and with force, the actor's occupied habitation, vehicle, or place of business or employment;

(B) unlawfully and with force removed, or was attempting to remove unlawfully and with force, the actor from the actor's habitation, vehicle, or place of business or employment; or

(C) was committing or attempting to commit an offense described by Subsection (a)(2)(B);

(2) did not provoke the person against whom the force was used; and

(3) was not otherwise engaged in criminal activity, other than a Class C misdemeanor that is a violation of a law or ordinance regulating traffic at the time the force was used.

(c) A person who has a right to be present at the location where the deadly force is used, who has not provoked the person against whom the deadly force is used, and who is not engaged in criminal activity at the time the deadly force is used is not required to retreat before using deadly force as described by this section.

(d) For purposes of Subsection (a)(2), in determining whether an actor described by Subsection (c) reasonably believed that the use of deadly force was necessary, a finder of fact may not consider whether the actor failed to retreat.

Last amended by Acts 2007, 80th Leg., R.S., Ch. 1 (S.B. 378), Sec. 3, eff. Sept. 1, 2007.

PC §9.33. DEFENSE OF THIRD PERSON.

A person is justified in using force or deadly force against another to protect a third person if:

(1) under the circumstances as the actor reasonably believes them to be, the actor would be justified under Section 9.31 or 9.32 in using force or deadly force to protect himself against the unlawful force or unlawful deadly force he reasonably believes to be threatening the third person he seeks to protect; and

(2) the actor reasonably believes that his intervention is immediately necessary to protect the third person.

Last amended by Acts 1993, 73rd Leg., ch. 900, Sec. 1.01, eff. Sept. 1, 1994.

PC §9.34. PROTECTION OF LIFE OR HEALTH.

(a) A person is justified in using force, but not deadly force, against another when and to the degree he reasonably believes the force is immediately necessary to prevent the other from committing suicide or inflicting serious bodily injury to himself.

(b) A person is justified in using both force and deadly force against another when and to the degree he reasonably believes the force or deadly force is immediately necessary to preserve the other's life in an emergency.

Last amended by Acts 1993, 73rd Leg., ch. 900, Sec. 1.01, eff. Sept. 1, 1994.

Subchapter D. PROTECTION OF PROPERTY

PC §9.41. PROTECTION OF ONE'S OWN PROPERTY.

(a) A person in lawful possession of land or tangible, movable property is justified in using force against another when and to the degree the actor reasonably believes the force is immediately necessary to prevent or terminate the other's trespass on the land or unlawful interference with the property.

(b) A person unlawfully dispossessed of land or tangible, movable property by another is justified in using force against the other when and to the degree the actor reasonably believes the force is immediately necessary to reenter the land or recover the property if the actor uses the force immediately or in fresh pursuit after the dispossession and:

    (1) the actor reasonably believes the other had no claim of right when he dispossessed the actor; or

    (2) the other accomplished the dispossession by using force, threat, or fraud against the actor.

Last amended by Acts 1993, 73rd Leg., ch. 900, Sec. 1.01, eff. Sept. 1, 1994.

PC §9.42. DEADLY FORCE TO PROTECT PROPERTY. A person is justified in using deadly force against another to protect land or tangible, movable property:

    (1) if he would be justified in using force against the other under Section 9.41; and

    (2) when and to the degree he reasonably believes the deadly force is immediately necessary:

        (A) to prevent the other's imminent commission of arson, burglary, robbery, aggravated robbery, theft during the nighttime, or criminal mischief during the nighttime; or

        (B) to prevent the other who is fleeing immediately after committing burglary, robbery, aggravated robbery, or theft during the night¬time from escaping with the property; and

    (3) he reasonably believes that:

        (A) the land or property cannot be protected or recovered by any other means; or

        (B) the use of force other than deadly force to protect or recover the land or property would expose the actor or another to a substantial risk of death or serious bodily injury.

Last amended by Acts 1993, 73rd Leg., ch. 900, Sec. 1.01, eff. Sept. 1, 1994.

PC §9.43. PROTECTION OF THIRD PERSON'S PROPERTY. A person is justified in using force or deadly force against another to protect land or tangible, movable property of a third person if, under the circumstances as he reasonably believes them to be, the actor would be justified under Section 9.41 or 9.42 in using force or deadly force to protect his own land or property and:

(1) the actor reasonably believes the unlawful interference constitutes attempted or consummated theft of or criminal mischief to the tangible movable property; or

(2) the actor reasonably believes that:

(A) the third person has requested his protection of the land or property;

(B) he has a legal duty to protect the third person's land or property; or

(C) the third person whose land or property he uses force or deadly force to protect is the actor's spouse, parent, or child, resides with the actor, or is under the actor's care.

Last amended by Acts 1993, 73rd Leg., ch. 900, Sec. 1.01, eff. Sept. 1, 1994.

PC §9.44. USE OF DEVICE TO PROTECT PROPERTY. The justification afforded by Sections 9.41 and 9.43 applies to the use of a device to protect land or tangible, movable property if:

(1) the device is not designed to cause, or known by the actor to create a substantial risk of causing, death or serious bodily injury; and

(2) use of the device is reasonable under all the circumstances as the actor reasonably believes them to be when he installs the device.

Last amended by Acts 1993, 73rd Leg., ch. 900, Sec. 1.01, eff. Sept.. 1, 1994.

Subchapter F. SPECIAL RELATIONSHIPS

PC §9.61. PARENT-CHILD.

(a) The use of force, but not deadly force, against a child younger than 18 years is justified:

(1) if the actor is the child's parent or stepparent or is acting in loco parentis to the child; and

(2) when and to the degree the actor reasonably believes the force is necessary to discipline the child or to safeguard or promote his welfare.

(b) For purposes of this section, "in loco parentis" includes grandparent and guardian, any person acting by, through, or under the direction of a court with jurisdiction over the child, and anyone who has express or implied consent of the parent or parents.

Last amended by Acts 1993, 73rd Leg., ch. 900, Sec. 1.01, eff. Sept. 1, 1994.

PC §9.62. EDUCATOR-STUDENT. The use of force, but not deadly force, against a person is justified:

(1) if the actor is entrusted with the care, supervision, or administration of the person for a special purpose; and

(2) when and to the degree the actor reasonably believes the force is necessary to further the special purpose or to maintain discipline in a group.

Last amended by Acts 1993, 73rd Leg., ch. 900, Sec. 1.01, eff. Sept. 1, 1994.

PC §9.63. GUARDIAN-INCOMPETENT. The use of force, but not deadly force, against a mental incompetent is justified:

(1) if the actor is the incompetent's guardian or someone similarly responsible for the general care and supervision of the incompetent; and

(2) when and to the degree the actor reasonably believes the force is necessary:

(A) to safeguard and promote the incompetent's welfare; or

(B) if the incompetent is in an institution for his care and custody, to maintain discipline in the institution.

Last amended by Acts 1993, 73rd Leg., ch. 900, Sec. 1.01, eff. Sept. 1, 1994.

Chapter 30. CRIMINAL TRESPASS

PC §30.05. CRIMINAL TRESPASS.

(a) A person commits an offense if the person enters or remains on or in property of another, including residential land, agricultural land, a recreational vehicle park, a building, or an aircraft or other vehicle, without effective consent and the person:

(1) had notice that the entry was forbidden; or

(2) received notice to depart but failed to do so.

(b) For purposes of this section:

(1) "Entry" means the intrusion of the entire body.

(2) "Notice" means:

(A) oral or written communication by the owner or someone with apparent authority to act for the owner;

(B) fencing or other enclosure obviously designed to exclude intruders or to contain livestock;

(C) a sign or signs posted on the property or at the entrance to the building, reasonably likely to come to the attention of intruders, indicating that entry is forbidden;

(D) the placement of identifying purple paint marks on trees or posts on the property, provided that the marks are:

(i) vertical lines of not less than eight inches in length and not less than one inch in width;

(ii) placed so that the bottom of the mark is not less than three feet from the ground or more than five feet from the ground; and

(iii) placed at locations that are readily visible to any person approaching the property and no more than:

(I) 100 feet apart on forest land; or

(II) 1,000 feet apart on land other than forest land; or

(E) the visible presence on the property of a crop grown for human consumption that is under cultivation, in the process of being harvested, or marketable if harvested at the time of entry.

(3) "Shelter center" has the meaning assigned by Section 51.002, Human Resources Code.

(4) "Forest land" means land on which the trees are potentially valuable for timber products.

(5) "Agricultural land" has the meaning assigned by Section 75.001, Civil Practice and Remedies Code.

(6) "Superfund site" means a facility that:

(A) is on the National Priorities List established under Section 105 of the federal Comprehensive Environmental Response, Compensation, and Liability Act of 1980 (42 U.S.C. Section 9605); or

(B) is listed on the state registry established under Section 361.181, Health and Safety Code.

(7) "Critical infrastructure facility" means one of the following, if completely enclosed by a fence or other physical barrier that is obviously designed to exclude intruders:

(A) a chemical manufacturing facility;

(B) a refinery;

(C) an electrical power generating facility, substation, switching station, electrical control center, or electrical transmission or distribution facility;

(D) a water intake structure, water treatment facility, waste-water treatment plant, or pump station;

(E) a natural gas transmission compressor station;

(F) a liquid natural gas terminal or storage facility;

(G) a telecommunications central switching office;

(H) a port, railroad switching yard, trucking terminal, or other freight transportation facility;

(I) a gas processing plant, including a plant used in the processing, treatment, or fractionation of natural gas; or

(J) a transmission facility used by a federally licensed radio or television station.

(8) "Protected freshwater area" has the meaning assigned by Section 90.001, Parks and Wildlife Code.

(9) "Recognized state" means another state with which the attorney general of this state, with the approval of the governor of this state, negotiated an agreement after determining that the other state:

(A) has firearm proficiency requirements for peace officers; and

(B) fully recognizes the right of peace officers commissioned in this state to carry weapons in the other state.

(10) "Recreational vehicle park" means a tract of land that has rental spaces for two or more recreational vehicles, as defined by Section 522.004, Transportation Code.

(11) "Residential land" means real property improved by a dwelling and zoned for or otherwise authorized for single-family or multifamily use.

(c) *[as repealed by Acts Effective Sept. 1, 2009, 81ˢᵗ Leg., R.S., HB 2609 §4.]

(d) An offense under this section is:

(1) a Class B misdemeanor, except as provided by Subdivisions (2) and (3);

(2) a Class C misdemeanor, except as provided by Subdivision (3), if the offense is committed:

(A) on agricultural land and within 100 feet of the boundary of the land; or

(B) on residential land and within 100 feet of a protected fresh-water area; and

(3) a Class A misdemeanor if:

(A) the offense is committed:

(i) in a habitation or a shelter center;

(ii) on a Superfund site; or

(iii) on or in a critical infrastructure facility; or

(B) the person carries a deadly weapon during the commission of the offense.

(e) It is a defense to prosecution under this section that the actor at the time of the offense was:

(1) a firefighter or emergency medical services personnel, as defined by Section 773.003, Health and Safety Code, acting in the lawful discharge of an official duty under exigent circumstances;

(2) a person who was:

(A) an employee or agent of:

(i) an electric utility, as defined by Section 31.002, Utilities Code;

(ii) a telecommunications provider, as defined by Section 51.002, Utilities Code;

(iii) a video service provider or cable service provider, as defined by Section 66.002, Utilities Code;

(iv) a gas utility, as defined by Section 101.003 or 121.001, Utilities Code; or

(v) a pipeline used for the transportation or sale of oil, gas, or related products; and

(B) performing a duty within the scope of that employment or agency; or

(3) a person who was:

(A) employed by or acting as agent for an entity that had, or that the person reasonably believed had, effective consent or authorization provided by law to enter the property; and

(B) performing a duty within the scope of that employment or agency.

(f) It is a defense to prosecution under this section that:

(1) the basis on which entry on the property or land or in the building was forbidden is that entry with a handgun was forbidden; and

(2) the person was carrying a concealed handgun and a license issued under Subchapter H, Chapter 411, Government Code, to carry a concealed handgun.

(g) It is a defense to prosecution under this section that the actor entered a railroad switching yard or any part of a railroad switching yard and was at that time an employee or a representative of employees exercising a right under the Railway Labor Act *(45 U.S.C. Section 151 et seq.).*

(h) At the punishment stage of a trial in which the attorney representing the state seeks the increase in punishment provided by Subsection (d)(1)(C), the defendant may raise the issue as to whether the defendant entered or remained on or in a critical infrastructure facility as part of a peaceful or lawful assembly, including an attempt to exercise rights guaranteed by state or federal labor laws. If the defendant proves the issue in the affirmative by a preponderance of the evidence, the increase in punishment provided by Subsection (d)(1)(C) does not apply.

(i) This section does not apply if:

(1) the basis on which entry on the property or land or in the building was forbidden is that entry with a handgun or other weapon was forbidden; and

(2) the actor at the time of the offense was a peace officer, including a commissioned peace officer of a recognized state, or a special investigator under Article 2.122, Code of Criminal Procedure, regardless of whether the peace officer or special investigator was engaged in the actual discharge of an official duty while carrying the weapon.

(j) *[as repealed by Acts effective Sept. 1, 2009, 81st Leg., R.S., HB 2609 §4.]*

Last amended by Acts 2013, 83rd Leg., R.S., Ch. 1302 (H.B. 3142), Sec. 12, eff. June 14, 2013.

PC §30.06. TRESPASS BY HOLDER OF LICENSE TO CARRY CONCEALED HANDGUN.

Text of section effective on Jan. 1, 2016

a) A license holder commits an offense if the license holder:
(1) carries a concealed handgun under the authority of Subchapter H, Chapter 411, Government Code, on property of another without effective consent; and
(2) received notice that entry on the property by a license holder with a concealed handgun was forbidden.
(b) For purposes of this section, a person receives notice if the owner of the property or someone with apparent authority to act for the owner provides notice to the person by oral or written communication.
(c) In this section:
(1) "Entry" has the meaning assigned by Section 30.05(b).
(2) "License holder" has the meaning assigned by Section 46.035(f).
(3) "Written communication" means:
(A) a card or other document on which is written language identical to the following: "Pursuant to Section 30.06, Penal Code (trespass by license holder with a concealed handgun), a person licensed under Subchapter H, Chapter 411, Government Code (handgun licensing law), may not enter this property with a concealed handgun"; or
(B) a sign posted on the property that:
(i) includes the language described by Paragraph (A) in both English and Spanish;
(ii) appears in contrasting colors with block letters at least one inch in height; and
(iii) is displayed in a conspicuous manner clearly visible to the public.
(d) An offense under this section is a Class C misdemeanor punishable by a fine not to exceed $200, except that the offense is a Class A misdemeanor if it is shown on the trial of the offense that, after entering the property, the license holder was personally given the notice by oral communication described by Subsection (b) and subsequently failed to depart.
(e) It is an exception to the application of this section that the property on which the license holder carries a handgun is owned or leased by a governmental entity and is not a premises or other place on which the license holder is prohibited from carrying the handgun under Section 46.03 or 46.035.

Added by Acts 1997, 75th Leg., ch. 1261, Sec. 23, eff. Sept. 1, 1997. Amended by Acts 1999, 76th Leg., ch. 62, Sec. 9.24, eff. Sept. 1, 1999; Acts 2003, 78th Leg., ch. 1178, Sec. 2, eff. Sept. 1, 2003.
Amended by:
Acts 2015, 84th Leg., R.S., Ch. 437 (H.B. 910), Sec. 41, eff. Jan. 1, 2016.
Acts 2015, 84th Leg., R.S., Ch. 437 (H.B. 910), Sec. 42, eff. Jan. 1, 2016.
Acts 2015, 84th Leg., R.S., Ch. 437 (H.B. 910), Sec. 43, eff. Jan. 1, 2016.

PC §30.07. TRESPASS BY LICENSE HOLDER WITH AN OPENLY CARRIED HANDGUN.

Text of section effective on Jan. 1, 2016

(a) A license holder commits an offense if the license holder:
(1) openly carries a handgun under the authority of Subchapter H, Chapter

411, Government Code, on property of another without effective consent; and

(2) received notice that entry on the property by a license holder openly carrying a handgun was forbidden.

(b) For purposes of this section, a person receives notice if the owner of the property or someone with apparent authority to act for the owner provides notice to the person by oral or written communication.

(c) In this section:

(1) "Entry" has the meaning assigned by Section 30.05(b).

(2) "License holder" has the meaning assigned by Section 46.035(f).

(3) "Written communication" means:

(A) a card or other document on which is written language identical to the following: "Pursuant to Section 30.07, Penal Code (trespass by license holder with an openly carried handgun), a person licensed under Subchapter H, Chapter 411, Government Code (handgun licensing law), may not enter this property with a handgun that is carried openly"; or

(B) a sign posted on the property that:

(i) includes the language described by Paragraph (A) in both English and Spanish;

(ii) appears in contrasting colors with block letters at least one inch in height; and

(iii) is displayed in a conspicuous manner clearly visible to the public at each entrance to the property.

(d) An offense under this section is a Class C misdemeanor punishable by a fine not to exceed $200, except that the offense is a Class A misdemeanor if it is shown on the trial of the offense that, after entering the property, the license holder was personally given the notice by oral communication described by Subsection (b) and subsequently failed to depart.

(e) It is an exception to the application of this section that the property on which the license holder openly carries the handgun is owned or leased by a governmental entity and is not a premises or other place on which the license holder is prohibited from carrying the handgun under Section 46.03 or 46.035.

(f) It is not a defense to prosecution under this section that the handgun was carried in a shoulder or belt holster.

Added by Acts 2015, 84th Leg., R.S., Ch. 437 (H.B. 910), Sec. 44, eff. Jan. 1, 2016.

Chapter 38. OBSTRUCTING A GOVERNMENTAL OPERATION

PC §38.01. DEFINITIONS. In this chapter:

(1) "Custody" means:

(A) under arrest by a peace officer or under restraint by a public servant pursuant to an order of a court of this state or another state of the United States; or

(B) under restraint by an agent or employee of a facility that is operated by or under contract with the United States and that confines persons arrested for, charged with, or convicted of criminal offenses.

(2) "Escape" means unauthorized departure from custody or failure to return to custody following temporary leave for a specific purpose or limited period or leave that is part of an intermittent sentence, but does not include a violation of conditions of community supervision or parole other than conditions that impose a period of confinement in a secure correctional facility.

Last amended by Acts 1997, 75th Leg., ch. 293, Sec. 2, eff. Sept. 1, 1997; Acts 1997, 75th Leg., ch. 750, Sec. 1, eff. Sept. 1, 1997.

Chapter 42. DISORDERLY CONDUCT AND RELATED OFFENSES

PC §42.01. DISORDERLY CONDUCT.

(a) A person commits an offense if he intentionally or knowingly:

(1) uses abusive, indecent, profane, or vulgar language in a public place, and the language by its very utterance tends to incite an immediate breach of the peace;

(2) makes an offensive gesture or display in a public place, and the gesture or display tends to incite an immediate breach of the peace;

(3) creates, by chemical means, a noxious and unreasonable odor in a public place;

(4) abuses or threatens a person in a public place in an obviously offensive manner;

(5) makes unreasonable noise in a public place other than a sport shooting range, as defined by Section 250.001, Local Government Code, or in or near a private residence that he has no right to occupy;

(6) fights with another in a public place;

(7) discharges a firearm in a public place other than a public road or a sport shooting range, as defined by Section 250.001, Local Government Code;

(8) displays a firearm or other deadly weapon in a public place in a manner calculated to alarm;

(9) discharges a firearm on or across a public road;

(10) exposes his anus or genitals in a public place and is reckless about whether another may be present who will be offended or alarmed by his act; or

(11) for a lewd or unlawful purpose:

(A) enters on the property of another and looks into a dwelling on the property through any window or other opening in the dwelling;

(B) while on the premises of a hotel or comparable establishment, looks into a guest room not the person's own through a window or other opening in the room; or

(C) while on the premises of a public place, looks into an area such as a restroom or shower stall or changing or dressing room that is designed to provide privacy to a person using the area.

(a-1) For purposes of Subsection (a), the term "public place" includes a public school campus or the school grounds on which a public school is located.

(b) It is a defense to prosecution under Subsection (a)(4) that the actor had significant provocation for his abusive or threatening conduct.

(c) For purposes of this section:

(1) an act is deemed to occur in a public place or near a private residence if it produces its offensive or proscribed consequences in the public place or near a private residence; and

(2) a noise is presumed to be unreasonable if the noise exceeds a decibel level of 85 after the person making the noise receives notice from a magistrate or peace officer that the noise is a public nuisance.

(d) An offense under this section is a Class C misdemeanor unless committed under Subsection (a)(7) or (a)(8), in which event it is a Class B misdemeanor.

(e) It is a defense to prosecution for an offense under Subsection (a)(7) or (9) that the person who discharged the firearm had a reasonable fear of bodily injury to the person or to another by a dangerous wild animal as defined by Section 822.101, Health and Safety Code.

(f) Subsections (a)(1), (2), (3), (5), and (6) do not apply to a person who, at the time the person engaged in conduct prohibited under the applicable subdivision, was a student younger than 12 years of age, and the prohibited conduct occurred at a public school campus during regular school hours.

(g) Noise arising from space flight activities, as defined by Section 100A.001, Civil Practice and Remedies Code, if lawfully conducted, does not constitute "unreasonable noise" for purposes of this section.

Acts 1973, 63rd Leg., p. 883, ch. 399, Sec. 1, eff. Jan. 1, 1974. Amended by Acts 1977, 65th Leg., p. 181, ch. 89, Sec. 1, 2, eff. Aug. 29, 1977; Acts 1983, 68th Leg., p. 4641, ch. 800, Sec. 1, eff. Sept. 1, 1983; Acts 1991, 72nd Leg., ch. 145, Sec. 2, eff. Aug. 26, 1991; Acts 1993, 73rd Leg., ch. 900, Sec. 1.01, eff. Sept. 1, 1994; Acts 1995, 74th Leg., ch. 318, Sec. 14, eff. Sept. 1, 1995; Acts 2001, 77th Leg., ch. 54, Sec. 4, eff. Sept. 1, 2001; Acts 2003, 78th Leg., ch. 389, Sec. 1, eff. Sept. 1, 2003.
Amended by:
Acts 2011, 82nd Leg., R.S., Ch. 691 (H.B. 359), Sec. 6, eff. September 1, 2011.
Acts 2013, 83rd Leg., R.S., Ch. 953 (H.B. 1791), Sec. 6, eff. September 1, 2013.
Acts 2013, 83rd Leg., R.S., Ch. 1407 (S.B. 393), Sec. 19, eff. September 1, 2013.
Acts 2013, 83rd Leg., R.S., Ch. 1409 (S.B. 1114), Sec. 9, eff. September 1, 2013.

Chapter 46. WEAPONS

PC §46.01. DEFINITIONS. In this Chapter:
(1) "Club" means an instrument that is specially designed, made, or adapted for the purpose of inflicting serious bodily injury or death by striking a person with the instrument, and includes but is not limited to the following:
    (A) blackjack;
    (B) nightstick;
    (C) mace;
    (D) tomahawk.
(2) "Explosive weapon" means any explosive or incendiary bomb, grenade, rocket, or mine, that is designed, made, or adapted for the purpose of inflicting serious bodily injury, death, or substantial property damage, or for the principal purpose of causing such a loud report as to cause undue public alarm or terror, and includes a device designed, made, or adapted for delivery or shooting an explosive weapon.
(3) "Firearm" means any device designed, made, or adapted to expel a projectile through a barrel by using the energy generated by an explosion or burning substance or any device readily convertible to that use. Firearm does not include a firearm that may have, as an integral part, a folding knife blade or other characteristics of weapons made illegal by this chapter and that is:
    (A) an antique or curio firearm manufactured before 1899; or
    (B) a replica of an antique or curio firearm manufactured before 1899, but only if the replica does not use rim fire or center fire ammunition.
(4) "Firearm silencer" means any device designed, made, or adapted to muffle the report of a firearm.
(5) "Handgun" means any firearm that is designed, made, or adapted to be fired with one hand.
(6) "Illegal knife" means a:
    (A) knife with a blade over five and one-half inches;

(B) hand instrument designed to cut or stab another by being thrown;

(C) dagger, including but not limited to a dirk, stiletto, and poniard;

(D) bowie knife;

(E) sword; or

(F) spear.

(7) "Knife" means any bladed hand instrument that is capable of inflicting serious bodily injury or death by cutting or stabbing a person with the instrument.

(8) "Knuckles" means any instrument that consists of finger rings or guards made of a hard substance and that is designed, made, or adapted for the purpose of inflicting serious bodily injury or death by striking a person with a fist enclosed in the knuckles.

(9) "Machine gun" means any firearm that is capable of shooting more than two shots automatically, without manual reloading, by a single function of the trigger.

(10) "Short-barrel firearm" means a rifle with a barrel length of less than 16 inches or a shotgun with a barrel length of less than 18 inches, or any weapon made from a shotgun or rifle if, as altered, it has an overall length of less than 26 inches.

(11) "Switchblade knife" means any knife that has a blade that folds, closes, or retracts into the handle or sheath and that opens automatically by pressure applied to a button or other device located on the handle or opens or releases a blade from the handle or sheath by the force of gravity or by the application of centrifugal force. The term does not include a knife that has a spring, detent, or other mechanism designed to create a bias toward closure and that requires exertion applied to the blade by hand, wrist, or arm to overcome the bias toward closure and open the knife.

(12) "Armor-piercing ammunition" means handgun ammunition that is designed primarily for the purpose of penetrating metal or body armor and to be used principally in pistols and revolvers.

(13) "Hoax bomb" means a device that:

(A) reasonably appears to be an explosive or incendiary device; or

(B) by its design causes alarm or reaction of any type by an official of a public safety agency or a volunteer agency organized to deal with emergencies.

(14) "Chemical dispensing device" means a device, other than a small chemical dispenser sold commercially for personal protection, that is designed, made, or adapted for the purpose of dispensing a substance capable of causing an adverse psychological or physiological effect on a human being.

(15) "Racetrack" has the meaning assigned that term by the Texas Racing Act (Article 179e, Vernon's Texas Civil Statutes).

(16) "Zip gun" means a device or combination of devices that was not originally a firearm and is adapted to expel a projectile through a smooth-bore or rifled-bore barrel by using the energy generated by an explosion or burning substance.

(17) "Tire deflation device" means a device, including a caltrop or spike strip, that, when driven over, impedes or stops the movement of a wheeled vehicle by puncturing one or more of the vehicle's tires. The term does not include a traffic control device that:

(A) is designed to puncture one or more of a vehicle's tires when driven over in a specific direction; and

(B) has a clearly visible sign posted in close proximity to the traffic control device that prohibits entry or warns motor vehicle operators of the traffic control device.

Last amended by Acts 2011, 82ⁿᵈ Leg., R.S., Ch. 920 (S.B. 1416), Sec. 1, eff. Sept. 1, 2011.

PC §46.02. UNLAWFUL CARRYING WEAPONS.

(a) A person commits an offense if the person intentionally, knowingly, or recklessly carries on or about his or her person a handgun, illegal knife, or club if the person is not:

(1) on the person's own premises or premises under the person's control; or

(2) inside of or directly en route to a motor vehicle or watercraft that is owned by the person or under the person's control.

Text of subsection effective on Jan. 1, 2016

(a-1) A person commits an offense if the person intentionally, knowingly, or recklessly carries on or about his or her person a handgun in a motor vehicle or watercraft that is owned by the person or under the person's control at any time in which:

(1) the handgun is in plain view, unless the person is licensed to carry a handgun under Subchapter H, Chapter 411, Government Code, and the handgun is carried in a shoulder or belt holster; or

(2) the person is:

(A) engaged in criminal activity, other than a Class C misdemeanor that is a violation of a law or ordinance regulating traffic or boating;

(B) prohibited by law from possessing a firearm; or

(C) a member of a criminal street gang, as defined by Section 71.01.

(a-2) For purposes of this section, "premises" includes real property and a recreational vehicle that is being used as living quarters, regardless of whether that use is temporary or permanent. In this subsection, "recreational vehicle" means a motor vehicle primarily designed as temporary living quarters or a vehicle that contains temporary living quarters and is designed to be towed by a motor vehicle. The term includes a travel trailer, camping trailer, truck camper, motor home, and horse trailer with living quarters.

(a-3) For purposes of this section, "watercraft" means any boat, motorboat, vessel, or personal watercraft, other than a seaplane on water, used or capable of being used for transportation on water.

(b) Except as provided by Subsection (c), an offense under this section is a Class A misdemeanor.

(c) An offense under this section is a felony of the third degree if the offense is committed on any premises licensed or issued a permit by this state for the sale of alcoholic beverages.

Acts 1973, 63ʳᵈ Leg., p. 883, ch. 399, Sec. 1, eff. Jan. 1, 1974. Amended by Acts 1975, 64ᵗʰ Leg., p. 109, ch. 49, Sec. 1, eff. April 15, 1975; Acts 1975, 64ᵗʰ Leg., p. 918, ch. 342, Sec. 14, eff. Sept. 1, 1975; Acts 1975, 64ᵗʰ Leg., p. 1330, ch. 494, Sec. 2, eff. June 19, 1975; Acts 1977, 65ᵗʰ Leg., p. 1879, ch. 746, Sec. 26, eff. Aug. 29, 1977; Acts 1981, 67ᵗʰ Leg., p. 2273, ch. 552, Sec. 1, eff. Aug. 31, 1981; Acts 1983, 68ᵗʰ Leg., p. 5113, ch. 931, Sec. 1, eff. Aug. 29, 1983; Acts 1987, 70ᵗʰ Leg., ch. 262, Sec. 21, eff. Sept. 1, 1987; Acts 1987, 70ᵗʰ Leg., ch. 873, Sec. 25, eff. Sept. 1, 1987; Acts 1991, 72ⁿᵈ Leg., ch. 168, Sec. 1, eff. Sept. 1, 1991. Redesignated from Penal Code Sec. 46.02, 46.03 and amended by Acts 1993, 73ʳᵈ Leg., ch. 900, Sec. 1.01, eff. Sept. 1, 1994. Amended by Acts 1995, 74ᵗʰ Leg., ch. 229, Sec. 2, eff. Sept. 1, 1995; Acts 1995, 74ᵗʰ Leg., ch. 318, Sec. 16, eff. Sept. 1, 1995; Acts 1995, 74ᵗʰ Leg., ch. 754, Sec. 15, eff. Sept. 1, 1995; Acts 1995, 74ᵗʰ Leg., ch. 790, Sec. 16, eff. Sept. 1, 1995; Acts 1995, 74ᵗʰ Leg., ch. 998, Sec. 3, eff. Sept. 1, 1995; Acts 1997, 75ᵗʰ Leg., ch. 165, Sec. 10.02, eff. Sept. 1, 1997; Acts 1997, 75ᵗʰ Leg., ch. 1221, Sec. 1, eff.

June 20, 1997; Acts 1997, 75th Leg., ch. 1261, Sec. 24, eff. Sept. 1, 1997.
Amended by:
Acts 2007, 80th Leg., R.S., Ch. 693 (H.B. 1815), Sec. 1, eff. Sept. 1, 2007.
Acts 2011, 82nd Leg., R.S., Ch. 679 (H.B. 25), Sec. 1, eff. Sept. 1, 2011.
Acts 2015, 84th Leg., R.S., Ch. 437 (H.B. 910), Sec. 45, eff. Jan. 1, 2016.

PC §46.03. PLACES WEAPONS PROHIBITED.

Text of subsection effective until Aug. 1, 2016

(a) A person commits an offense if the person intentionally, knowingly, or recklessly possesses or goes with a firearm, illegal knife, club, or prohibited weapon listed in Section 46.05(a):

(1) on the physical premises of a school or educational institution, any grounds or building on which an activity sponsored by a school or educational institution is being conducted, or a passenger transportation vehicle of a school or educational institution, whether the school or educational institution is public or private, unless pursuant to written regulations or written authorization of the institution;

(2) on the premises of a polling place on the day of an election or while early voting is in progress;

(3) on the premises of any government court or offices utilized by the court, unless pursuant to written regulations or written authorization of the court;

(4) on the premises of a racetrack;

(5) in or into a secured area of an airport; or

(6) within 1,000 feet of premises the location of which is designated by the Texas Department of Criminal Justice as a place of execution under Article 43.19, Code of Criminal Procedure, on a day that a sentence of death is set to be imposed on the designated premises and the person received notice that:

(A) going within 1,000 feet of the premises with a weapon listed under this subsection was prohibited; or

(B) possessing a weapon listed under this subsection within 1,000 feet of the premises was prohibited.

Text of subsection effective on Aug. 1, 2016

(a) A person commits an offense if the person intentionally, knowingly, or recklessly possesses or goes with a firearm, illegal knife, club, or prohibited weapon listed in Section 46.05(a):

(1) on the physical premises of a school or educational institution, any grounds or building on which an activity sponsored by a school or educational institution is being conducted, or a passenger transportation vehicle of a school or educational institution, whether the school or educational institution is public or private, unless:

(A) pursuant to written regulations or written authorization of the institution; or

(B) the person possesses or goes with a concealed handgun that the person is licensed to carry under Subchapter H, Chapter 411, Government Code, and no other weapon to which this section applies, on the premises of an institution of higher education or private or independent institution of higher education, on any grounds or building on which an activity sponsored by the institution is being conducted, or in a passenger transportation vehicle of the institution;

(2) on the premises of a polling place on the day of an election or while early voting is in progress;

(3) on the premises of any government court or offices utilized by the court, unless pursuant to written regulations or written authorization of the court;

(4) on the premises of a racetrack;

(5) in or into a secured area of an airport; or

(6) within 1,000 feet of premises the location of which is designated by the Texas Department of Criminal Justice as a place of execution under Article 43.19, Code of Criminal Procedure, on a day that a sentence of death is set to be imposed on the designated premises and the person received notice that:

(A) going within 1,000 feet of the premises with a weapon listed under this subsection was prohibited; or

(B) possessing a weapon listed under this subsection within 1,000 feet of the premises was prohibited.

(b) It is a defense to prosecution under Subsections (a)(1)-(4) that the actor possessed a firearm while in the actual discharge of his official duties as a member of the armed forces or national guard or a guard employed by a penal institution, or an officer of the court.

Text of subsection effective until Aug. 1, 2016

(c) In this section:

(1) "Premises" has the meaning assigned by Section 46.035.

(2) "Secured area" means an area of an airport terminal building to which access is controlled by the inspection of persons and property under federal law.

Text of subsection effective on Aug. 1, 2016

(c) In this section:

(1) "Institution of higher education" and "private or independent institution of higher education" have the meanings assigned by Section 61.003, Education Code.

(2) "Premises" has the meaning assigned by Section 46.035.

(3) "Secured area" means an area of an airport terminal building to which access is controlled by the inspection of persons and property under federal law.

(d) It is a defense to prosecution under Subsection (a)(5) that the actor possessed a firearm or club while traveling to or from the actor's place of assignment or in the actual discharge of duties as:

(1) a member of the armed forces or national guard;

(2) a guard employed by a penal institution; or

(3) a security officer commissioned by the Texas Private Security Board if:

(A) the actor is wearing a distinctive uniform; and

(B) the firearm or club is in plain view; or

(4) a security officer who holds a personal protection authorization under Chapter 1702, Occupations Code, provided that the officer is either:

(A) wearing the uniform of a security officer, including any uniform or apparel described by Section 1702.323(d), Occupations Code, and carrying the officer's firearm in plain view; or

(B) not wearing the uniform of a security officer and carrying the officer's firearm in a concealed manner.

(e) It is a defense to prosecution under Subsection (a)(5) that the actor checked all firearms as baggage in accordance with federal or state law or regulations before entering a secured area.

(e-1) It is a defense to prosecution under Subsection (a)(5) that the actor:

(1) possessed, at the screening checkpoint for the secured area, a concealed handgun that the actor was licensed to carry under Subchapter H, Chapter 411, Government Code; and

(2) exited the screening checkpoint for the secured area immediately upon completion of the required screening processes and notification that the actor possessed the handgun.

(e-2) A peace officer investigating conduct that may constitute an offense under Subsection (a)(5) and that consists only of an actor's possession of a concealed handgun that the actor is licensed to carry under Subchapter H, Chapter 411, Government Code, may not arrest the actor for the offense unless:

(1) the officer advises the actor of the defense available under Subsection (e-1) and gives the actor an opportunity to exit the screening checkpoint for the secured area; and

(2) the actor does not immediately exit the checkpoint upon completion of the required screening processes.

Text of subsection as amended by Acts 2015, 84th Leg., R.S., Ch. 1001 (H.B. 554), Sec. 1

(f) Except as provided by Subsection (e-1), it is not a defense to prosecution under this section that the actor possessed a handgun and was licensed to carry a concealed handgun under Subchapter H, Chapter 411, Government Code.

*Text of subsection as amended by Acts 2015, 84th Leg., R.S., Ch. 437 (H.B. 910), Sec. 46
Text of subsection effective on Jan. 1, 2016*

(f) It is not a defense to prosecution under this section that the actor possessed a handgun and was licensed to carry a handgun under Subchapter H, Chapter 411, Government Code.

(g) An offense under this section is a third degree felony.

(h) It is a defense to prosecution under Subsection (a)(4) that the actor possessed a firearm or club while traveling to or from the actor's place of assignment or in the actual discharge of duties as a security officer commissioned by the Texas Board of Private Investigators and Private Security Agencies, if:

(1) the actor is wearing a distinctive uniform; and

(2) the firearm or club is in plain view.

(i) It is an exception to the application of Subsection (a)(6) that the actor possessed a firearm or club:

(1) while in a vehicle being driven on a public road; or

(2) at the actor's residence or place of employment.

Acts 1973, 63rd Leg., p. 883, ch. 399, Sec. 1, eff. Jan. 1, 1974. Amended by Acts 1983, 68th Leg., p. 2962, ch. 508, Sec. 1, eff. Aug. 29, 1983; Acts 1989, 71st Leg., ch. 749, Sec. 2, eff. Sept. 1, 1989; Acts 1991, 72nd Leg., ch. 203, Sec. 2.79; Acts 1991, 72nd Leg., ch. 386, Sec. 71, eff. Aug. 26, 1991; Acts 1991, 72nd Leg., ch. 433, Sec. 1, eff. Sept. 1, 1991; Acts 1991, 72nd Leg., ch. 554, Sec. 50, eff. Sept. 1, 1991. Renumbered from Penal Code Sec. 46.04 and amended by Acts 1993, 73rd Leg., ch. 900, Sec. 1.01, eff. Sept. 1, 1994. Amended by Acts 1995, 74th Leg., ch. 229, Sec. 3, eff. Sept. 1, 1995; Acts 1995, 74th Leg., ch. 260, Sec. 42, eff. May 30, 1995; Acts 1995, 74th Leg., ch. 318, Sec. 17, eff. Sept. 1, 1995; Acts

1995, 74th Leg., ch. 790, Sec. 17, eff. Sept. 1, 1995; Acts 1997, 75th Leg., ch. 165, Sec. 10.03, 31.01(70), eff. Sept. 1, 1997; Acts 1997, 75th Leg., ch. 1043, Sec. 1, eff. Sept. 1, 1997; Acts 1997, 75th Leg., ch. 1221, Sec. 2, 3, eff. June 20, 1997; Acts 1997, 75th Leg., ch. 1261, Sec. 25, eff. Sept. 1, 1997; Acts 2001, 77th Leg., ch. 1060, Sec. 1, 2 eff. Sept. 1, 2001; Acts 2003, 78th Leg., ch. 1178, Sec. 3, eff. Sept. 1, 2003.
Amended by:
Acts 2009, 81st Leg., R.S., Ch. 1146 (H.B. 2730), Sec. 4B.21, eff. Sept. 1, 2009.
Acts 2015, 84th Leg., R.S., Ch. 437 (H.B. 910), Sec. 46, eff. Jan. 1, 2016.
Acts 2015, 84th Leg., R.S., Ch. 438 (S.B. 11), Sec. 3, eff. Aug. 1, 2016.
Acts 2015, 84th Leg., R.S., Ch. 1001 (H.B. 554), Sec. 1, eff. Sept. 1, 2015.

PC §46.035. UNLAWFUL CARRYING OF HANDGUN BY LICENSE HOLDER.

Text of subsection effective on Jan. 1, 2016

(a) A license holder commits an offense if the license holder carries a handgun on or about the license holder's person under the authority of Subchapter H, Chapter 411, Government Code, and intentionally displays the handgun in plain view of another person in a public place. It is an exception to the application of this subsection that the handgun was partially or wholly visible but was carried in a shoulder or belt holster by the license holder.

Text of subsection as added by Acts 2015, 84th Leg., R.S.,
Ch. 437 (H.B. 910), Sec. 47
Text of subsection effective on Jan. 1, 2016

(a-1) Notwithstanding Subsection (a), a license holder commits an offense if the license holder carries a partially or wholly visible handgun, regardless of whether the handgun is holstered, on or about the license holder's person under the authority of Subchapter H, Chapter 411, Government Code, and intentionally displays the handgun in plain view of another person:
  (1) on the premises of an institution of higher education or private or independent institution of higher education; or
  (2) on any public or private driveway, street, sidewalk or walkway, parking lot, parking garage, or other parking area of an institution of higher education or private or independent institution of higher education.

Text of subsection as added by Acts 2015, 84th Leg., R.S.,
Ch. 438 (S.B. 11), Sec. 4
Text of subsection effective on Aug. 1, 2016

(a-1) Notwithstanding Subsection (a), a license holder commits an offense if the license holder carries a partially or wholly visible handgun, regardless of whether the handgun is holstered, on or about the license holder's person under the authority of Subchapter H, Chapter 411, Government Code, and intentionally or knowingly displays the handgun in plain view of another person:
  (1) on the premises of an institution of higher education or private or independent institution of higher education; or
  (2) on any public or private driveway, street, sidewalk or walkway, parking lot, parking garage, or other parking area of an institution of higher education or private or independent institution of higher education.

Text of subsection effective on Aug. 1, 2016

(a-2) Notwithstanding Subsection (a) or Section 46.03(a), a license holder commits an offense if the license holder carries a handgun on the campus of a private or independent institution of higher education in this state that has established rules, regulations, or other provisions prohibiting license holders from carrying handguns pursuant to Section 411.2031(e), Government Code, or on the grounds or building on which an activity sponsored by such an institution is being conducted, or in a passenger transportation vehicle of such an institution, regardless of whether the handgun is concealed, provided the institution gives effective notice under Section 30.06.

Text of subsection effective on Aug. 1, 2016

(a-3) Notwithstanding Subsection (a) or Section 46.03(a), a license holder commits an offense if the license holder intentionally carries a concealed handgun on a portion of a premises located on the campus of an institution of higher education in this state on which the carrying of a concealed handgun is prohibited by rules, regulations, or other provisions established under Section 411.2031(d-1), Government Code, provided the institution gives effective notice under Section 30.06 with respect to that portion.

Text of subsection effective on Jan. 1, 2016

(b) A license holder commits an offense if the license holder intentionally, knowingly, or recklessly carries a handgun under the authority of Subchapter H, Chapter 411, Government Code, regardless of whether the handgun is concealed or carried in a shoulder or belt holster, on or about the license holder's person:

(1) on the premises of a business that has a permit or license issued under Chapter 25, 28, 32, 69, or 74, Alcoholic Beverage Code, if the business derives 51 percent or more of its income from the sale or service of alcoholic beverages for on-premises consumption, as determined by the Texas Alcoholic Beverage Commission under Section 104.06, Alcoholic Beverage Code;

(2) on the premises where a high school, collegiate, or professional sporting event or interscholastic event is taking place, unless the license holder is a participant in the event and a handgun is used in the event;

(3) on the premises of a correctional facility;

(4) on the premises of a hospital licensed under Chapter 241, Health and Safety Code, or on the premises of a nursing facility licensed under Chapter 242, Health and Safety Code, unless the license holder has written authorization of the hospital or nursing facility administration, as appropriate;

(5) in an amusement park; or

(6) on the premises of a church, synagogue, or other established place of religious worship.

(c) A license holder commits an offense if the license holder intentionally, knowingly, or recklessly carries a handgun under the authority of Subchapter H, Chapter 411, Government Code, regardless of whether the handgun is concealed or carried in a shoulder or belt holster, in the room or rooms where a meeting of a governmental entity is held and if the meeting is an open meeting subject to Chapter 551, Government Code, and the entity provided notice as required by that chapter.

Text of subsection effective on Jan. 1, 2016

(d) A license holder commits an offense if, while intoxicated, the license holder carries a handgun under the authority of Subchapter H, Chapter 411,

Government Code, regardless of whether the handgun is concealed or carried in a shoulder or belt holster.

(e) A license holder who is licensed as a security officer under Chapter 1702, Occupations Code, and employed as a security officer commits an offense if, while in the course and scope of the security officer's employment, the security officer violates a provision of Subchapter H, Chapter 411, Government Code.

(f) In this section:

(1) "Amusement park" means a permanent indoor or outdoor facility or park where amusement rides are available for use by the public that is located in a county with a population of more than one million, encompasses at least 75 acres in surface area, is enclosed with access only through controlled entries, is open for operation more than 120 days in each calendar year, and has security guards on the premises at all times. The term does not include any public or private driveway, street, sidewalk or walkway, parking lot, parking garage, or other parking area.

(1-a) "Institution of higher education" and "private or independent institution of higher education" have the meanings assigned by Section 61.003, Education Code.

(2) "License holder" means a person licensed to carry a handgun under Subchapter H, Chapter 411, Government Code.

(3) "Premises" means a building or a portion of a building. The term does not include any public or private driveway, street, sidewalk or walkway, parking lot, parking garage, or other parking area.

Text of subsection as amended by Acts 2015, 84ᵗʰ Leg., R.S.,
Ch. 437 (H.B. 910), Sec. 47
Text of subsection effective on Jan. 1, 2016

(g) An offense under this section is a Class A misdemeanor, unless the offense is committed under Subsection (b)(1) or (b)(3), in which event the offense is a felony of the third degree.

Text of subsection as amended by Acts 2015, 84ᵗʰ Leg., R.S.,
Ch. 438 (S.B. 11), Sec. 4
Text of subsection effective on Aug. 1, 2016

(g) An offense under Subsection (a), (a-1), (a-2), (a-3), (b), (c), (d), or (e) is a Class A misdemeanor, unless the offense is committed under Subsection (b)(1) or (b)(3), in which event the offense is a felony of the third degree.

Text of subsection as amended by Acts 2015, 84ᵗʰ Leg., R.S.,
Ch. 437 (H.B. 910), Sec. 47
Text of subsection effective on Jan. 1, 2016

(h) It is a defense to prosecution under Subsection (a) or (a-1) that the actor, at the time of the commission of the offense, displayed the handgun under circumstances in which the actor would have been justified in the use of force or deadly force under Chapter 9.

Text of subsection as amended by Acts 2015, 84ᵗʰ Leg., R.S.,
Ch. 438 (S.B. 11), Sec. 4
Text of subsection effective on Aug. 1, 2016

(h) It is a defense to prosecution under Subsection (a), (a-1), (a-2), or (a-3) that the actor, at the time of the commission of the offense, displayed the handgun under circumstances in which the actor would have been justified in the use of force or deadly force under Chapter 9.

Text of subsection as added by Acts 2007, 80th Leg., R.S.,
Ch. 1214 (H.B. 1889), Sec. 2

(h-1) It is a defense to prosecution under Subsections (b) and (c) that the actor, at the time of the commission of the offense, was:
   (1) an active judicial officer, as defined by Section 411.201, Government Code; or
   (2) a bailiff designated by the active judicial officer and engaged in escorting the officer.

Text of subsection as added by Acts 2007, 80th Leg., R.S.,
Ch. 1222 (H.B. 2300), Sec. 5

(h-1) It is a defense to prosecution under Subsections (b)(1), (2), and (4)-(6), and (c) that at the time of the commission of the offense, the actor was:
   (1) a judge or justice of a federal court;
   (2) an active judicial officer, as defined by Section 411.201, Government Code; or
   (3) a district attorney, assistant district attorney, criminal district attorney, assistant criminal district attorney, county attorney, or assistant county attorney.

Text of subsection effective on Jan. 1, 2016

(i) Subsections (b)(4), (b)(5), (b)(6), and (c) do not apply if the actor was not given effective notice under Section 30.06 or 30.07.

Text of subsection as amended by Acts 2015, 84th Leg., R.S.,
Ch. 437 (H.B. 910), Sec. 47
Text of subsection effective on Jan. 1, 2016

(j) Subsections (a), (a-1), and (b)(1) do not apply to a historical reenactment performed in compliance with the rules of the Texas Alcoholic Beverage Commission.

Text of subsection as amended by Acts 2015, 84th Leg., R.S.,
Ch. 438 (S.B. 11), Sec. 4
Text of subsection effective on Aug. 1, 2016

(j) Subsections (a), (a-1), (a-2), (a-3), and (b)(1) do not apply to a historical reenactment performed in compliance with the rules of the Texas Alcoholic Beverage Commission.
(k) It is a defense to prosecution under Subsection (b)(1) that the actor was not given effective notice under Section 411.204, Government Code.

Text of subsection effective on Aug. 1, 2016

(l) Subsection (b)(2) does not apply on the premises where a collegiate sporting event is taking place if the actor was not given effective notice under Section 30.06.

Added by Acts 1995, 74th Leg., ch. 229, Sec. 4, eff. Sept. 1, 1995. Amended by Acts 1997, 75th Leg., ch. 165, Sec. 10.04, eff. Sept. 1, 1997; Acts 1997, 75th Leg., ch. 1261, Sec. 26,

27, eff. Sept. 1, 1997; Acts 2001, 77ᵗʰ Leg., ch. 1420, Sec. 14.833, eff. Sept. 1, 2001.
Amended by:
Acts 2005, 79ᵗʰ Leg., Ch. 976 (H.B. 1813), Sec. 3, eff. Sept. 1, 2005.
Acts 2007, 80ᵗʰ Leg., R.S., Ch. 1214 (H.B. 1889), Sec. 2, eff. June 15, 2007.
Acts 2007, 80ᵗʰ Leg., R.S., Ch. 1222 (H.B. 2300), Sec. 5, eff. June 15, 2007.
Acts 2009, 81ˢᵗ Leg., R.S., Ch. 687 (H.B. 2664), Sec. 1, eff. Sept. 1, 2009.
Acts 2013, 83ʳᵈ Leg., R.S., Ch. 72 (S.B. 299), Sec. 1, eff. Sept. 1, 2013.
Acts 2015, 84ᵗʰ Leg., R.S., Ch. 437 (H.B. 910), Sec. 47, eff. Jan. 1, 2016.
Acts 2015, 84ᵗʰ Leg., R.S., Ch. 437 (H.B. 910), Sec. 48, eff. Jan. 1, 2016.
Acts 2015, 84ᵗʰ Leg., R.S., Ch. 438 (S.B. 11), Sec. 4, eff. Aug. 1, 2016.
Acts 2015, 84ᵗʰ Leg., R.S., Ch. 438 (S.B. 11), Sec. 5, eff. Aug. 1, 2016.
Acts 2015, 84ᵗʰ Leg., R.S., Ch. 593 (S.B. 273), Sec. 2, eff. Sept. 1, 2015.

PC §46.04. UNLAWFUL POSSESSION OF FIREARM.

(a) A person who has been convicted of a felony commits an offense if he possesses a firearm:

(1) after conviction and before the fifth anniversary of the person's release from confinement following conviction of the felony or the person's release from supervision under community supervision, parole, or mandatory supervision, whichever date is later; or

(2) after the period described by Subdivision (1), at any location other than the premises at which the person lives.

(b) A person who has been convicted of an offense under Section 22.01, punishable as a Class A misdemeanor and involving a member of the person's family or household, commits an offense if the person possesses a firearm before the fifth anniversary of the later of:

(1) the date of the person's release from confinement following conviction of the misdemeanor; or

(2) the date of the person's release from community supervision following conviction of the misdemeanor.

(c) A person, other than a peace officer, as defined by Section 1.07, actively engaged in employment as a sworn, full-time paid employee of a state agency or political subdivision, who is subject to an order issued under Section 6.504 or Chapter 85, Family Code, under Article 17.292 or Chapter 7A, Code of Criminal Procedure, or by another jurisdiction as provided by Chapter 88, Family Code, commits an offense if the person possesses a firearm after receiving notice of the order and before expiration of the order.

(d) In this section, "family," "household," and "member of a household" have the meanings assigned by Chapter 71, Family Code.

(e) An offense under Subsection (a) is a felony of the third degree. An offense under Subsection (b) or (c) is a Class A misdemeanor.

(f) For the purposes of this section, an offense under the laws of this state, another state, or the United States is, except as provided by Subsection (g), a felony if, at the time it is committed, the offense:

(1) is designated by a law of this state as a felony;

(2) contains all the elements of an offense designated by a law of this state as a felony; or

(3) is punishable by confinement for one year or more in a penitentiary.

(g) An offense is not considered a felony for purposes of Subsection (f) if, at the time the person possesses a firearm, the offense:

(1) is not designated by a law of this state as a felony; and

(2) does not contain all the elements of any offense designated by a law of this state as a felony.

Acts 1973, 63rd Leg., p. 883, ch. 399, Sec. 1, eff. Jan. 1, 1974. Renumbered from Penal Code Sec. 46.05 and amended by Acts 1993, 73rd Leg., ch. 900, Sec. 1.01, eff. Sept. 1, 1994. Amended by Acts 2001, 77th Leg., ch. 23, Sec. 2, eff. Sept. 1, 2001; Acts 2003, 78th Leg., ch. 836, Sec. 4, eff. Sept. 1, 2003.
Amended by:
Acts 2009, 81st Leg., R.S., Ch. 1146 (H.B. 2730), Sec. 11.24, eff. September 1, 2009.

PC §46.041 UNLAWFUL POSSESSION OF METAL OR BODY ARMOR BY FELON.

(a) In this section, "metal or body armor" means any body covering manifestly designed, made, or adapted for the purpose of protecting a person against gunfire.

(b) A person who has been convicted of a felony commits an offense if after the conviction the person possesses metal or body armor.

(c) An offense under this section is a felony of the third degree.

Added by Acts 2001, 77th Leg., ch. 452, Sec. 1, eff. Sept. 1, 2001.

PC §46.05. PROHIBITED WEAPONS. (a) A person commits an offense if the person intentionally or knowingly possesses, manufactures, transports, repairs, or sells:

(1) an explosive weapon;
(2) a machine gun;
(3) a short-barrel firearm;
(4) a firearm silencer;
(5) knuckles;
(6) armor-piercing ammunition;
(7) a chemical dispensing device;
(8) a zip gun; or
(9) a tire deflation device.

(b) It is a defense to prosecution under this section that the actor's conduct was incidental to the performance of official duty by the armed forces or national guard, a governmental law enforcement agency, or a correctional facility.

(c) It is a defense to prosecution under this section that the actor's possession was pursuant to registration pursuant to the National Firearms Act, as amended.

(d) It is an affirmative defense to prosecution under this section that the actor's conduct:

(1) was incidental to dealing with a short-barrel firearm or tire deflation device solely as an antique or curio;
(2) was incidental to dealing with armor-piercing ammunition solely for the purpose of making the ammunition available to an organization, agency, or institution listed in Subsection (b); or
(3) was incidental to dealing with a tire deflation device solely for the purpose of making the device available to an organization, agency, or institution listed in Subsection (b).

(e) An offense under Subsection (a)(1), (2), (3), (4), (6), (7), or (8) is a felony of the third degree. An offense under Subsection (a)(9) is a state jail felony. An offense under Subsection (a)(5) is a Class A misdemeanor.

(f) It is a defense to prosecution under this section for the possession of a chemical dispensing device that the actor is a security officer and has received training on the use of the chemical dispensing device by a training program that is:

    (1) provided by the Texas Commission on Law Enforcement; or

    (2) approved for the purposes described by this subsection by the Texas Private Security Board of the Department of Public Safety.

(g) In Subsection (f), "security officer" means a commissioned security officer as defined by Section 1702.002, Occupations Code, or a noncommissioned security officer registered under Section 1702.221, Occupations Code.

Last amended by Acts 2013, 83rd Leg., R.S., Ch. 960 (H.B. 1862), Sec. 1, eff. Sept. 1, 2013.

PC §46.10. DEADLY WEAPON IN PENAL INSTITUTION.

(a) A person commits an offense if, while confined in a penal institution, he intentionally, knowingly, or recklessly:

    (1) carries on or about his person a deadly weapon; or

    (2) possesses or conceals a deadly weapon in the penal institution.

(b) It is an affirmative defense to prosecution under this section that at the time of the offense the actor was engaged in conduct authorized by an employee of the penal institution.

(c) A person who is subject to prosecution under both this section and another section under this Chapter may be prosecuted under either section.

(d) An offense under this section is a felony of the third degree.

Renumbered from Penal Code Sec. 46.11 by Acts 1993, 73rd Leg., ch. 900, Sec. 1.01, eff. Sept. 1, 1994.

PC §46.13. MAKING A FIREARM ACCESSIBLE TO A CHILD.

(a) In this section:

    (1) "Child" means a person younger than 17 years of age.

    (2) "Readily dischargeable firearm" means a firearm that is loaded with ammunition, whether or not a round is in the chamber.

    (3) "Secure" means to take steps that a reasonable person would take to prevent the access to a readily dischargeable firearm by a child, including but not limited to placing a firearm in a locked container or temporarily rendering the firearm inoperable by a trigger lock or other means

(b) A person commits an offense if a child gains access to a readily dischargeable firearm and the person with criminal negligence:

    (1) failed to secure the firearm; or

    (2) left the firearm in a place to which the person knew or should have known the child would gain access.

(c) It is an affirmative defense to prosecution under this section that the child's access to the firearm:

    (1) was supervised by a person older than 18 years of age and was for hunting, sporting, or other lawful purposes;

    (2) consisted of lawful defense by the child of people or property;

    (3) was gained by entering property in violation of this code; or

    (4) occurred during a time when the actor was engaged in an agricultural enterprise.

(d) Except as provided by Subsection (e), an offense under this section is a Class C misdemeanor.

(e) An offense under this section is a Class A misdemeanor if the child discharges the firearm and causes death or serious bodily injury to himself or another person.

(f) A peace officer or other person may not arrest the actor before the seventh day after the date on which the offense is committed if:

(1) the actor is a member of the family, as defined by Section 71.003, Family Code, of the child who discharged the firearm; and

(2) the child in discharging the firearm caused the death of or serious injury to the child.

(g) A dealer of firearms shall post in a conspicuous position on the premises where the dealer conducts business a sign that contains the following warning in block letters not less than one inch in height:

"IT IS UNLAWFUL TO STORE, TRANSPORT, OR ABANDON AN UNSECURED FIREARM IN A PLACE WHERE CHILDREN ARE LIKELY TO BE AND CAN OBTAIN ACCESS TO THE FIREARM."

Last amended by Acts 1999, 76th Leg., ch. 62, Sec. 15.02(g), eff. Sept. 1, 1999.

PC §46.15. NON-APPLICABILITY.

(a) Sections 46.02 and 46.03 do not apply to a person who:

(1) peace officers or special investigators under Article 2.122, Code of Criminal Procedure, and neither section prohibits a peace officer or special investigator from carrying a weapon in this state, including in an establishment in this state serving the public, regardless of whether the peace officer or special investigator is engaged in the actual discharge of the officer's or investigator's duties while carrying the weapon;

(2) parole officers and neither section prohibits an officer from carrying a weapon in this state if the officer is:

(A) engaged in the actual discharge of the officer's duties while carrying the weapon; and

(B) in compliance with policies and procedures adopted by the Texas Department of Criminal Justice regarding the possession of a weapon by an officer while on duty;

(3) community supervision and corrections department officers appointed or employed under Section 76.004, Government Code, and neither section prohibits an officer from carrying a weapon in this state if the officer is:

(A) engaged in the actual discharge of the officer's duties while carrying the weapon; and

(B) authorized to carry a weapon under Section 76.0051, Government Code;

(4) an active judicial officer as defined by Section 411.201, Government Code, who is licensed to carry a concealed handgun under Subchapter H, Chapter 411, Government Code;

(5) an honorably retired peace officer, qualified retired law enforcement officer, federal criminal investigator or former reserve law enforcement officer who holds a certificate of proficiency issued under Section 1701.357, Occupations Code, and is carrying a photo identification that is issued by a federal, state, or local law enforcement agency, as applicable, and that:

(A) verifies the officer is an honorably retired peace officer;

(B) a qualified retired law enforcement officer;

(C) a federal criminal investigator; or

(D) a former reserve law enforcement officer who has served in that capacity not less than a total of 15 years with one or more state or local law enforcement agencies.

(6) a district attorney, criminal district attorney, county attorney, or municipal attorney who is licensed to carry a concealed handgun under Subchapter H, Chapter 411, Government Code;

(7) an assistant district attorney, assistant criminal district attorney, or assistant county attorney who is licensed to carry a concealed handgun under Subchapter H, Chapter 411, Government Code;

(8) a bailiff designated by an active judicial officer as defined by Section 411.201, Government Code, who is:

(A) licensed to carry a concealed handgun under Chapter 411, Government Code; and

(B) engaged in escorting the judicial officer; or

(9) a juvenile probation officer who is authorized to carry a firearm under Section 142.006, Human Resources Code.

(b) Section 46.02 does not apply to a person who:

(1) is in the actual discharge of official duties as a member of the armed forces or state military forces as defined by Section 431.001, Government Code, or as a guard employed by a penal institution;

(2) is traveling;

(3) is engaging in lawful hunting, fishing, or other sporting activity on the immediate premises where the activity is conducted, or is en route between the premises and the actor's residence, motor vehicle, or watercraft, if the weapon is a type commonly used in the activity;

(4) holds a security officer commission issued by the Texas Private Security Board, if the person is engaged in the performance of the person's duties as an officer commissioned under Chapter 1702, Occupations Code, or is traveling to or from the person's place of assignment and is wearing the officer's uniform and carrying the officer's weapon in plain view;

(5) acts as a personal protection officer and carries the person's security officer commission and personal protection officer authorization, if the person:

(A) is engaged in the performance of the person's duties as a personal protection officer under Chapter 1702, Occupations Code, or is traveling to or from the person's place of assignment; and

(B) is either:

(i) wearing the uniform of a security officer, including any uniform or apparel described by Section 1702.323(d), Occupations Code, and carrying the officer's weapon in plain view; or

(ii) not wearing the uniform of a security officer and carrying the officer's weapon in a concealed manner;

(6) is carrying a concealed handgun and a valid license issued under Subchapter H, Chapter 411, Government Code, to carry a concealed handgun;

(7) holds an alcoholic beverage permit or license or is an employee of a holder of an alcoholic beverage permit or license if the person is supervising the operation of the permitted or licensed premises; or

(8) is a student in a law enforcement class engaging in an activity required as part of the class, if the weapon is a type commonly used in the activity and the person is:

(A) on the immediate premises where the activity is conducted; or

(B) en route between those premises and the person's residence and is carrying the weapon unloaded.

(c) The provision of Section 46.02 prohibiting the carrying of a club does not apply to a noncommissioned security guard at an institution of higher education who carries a nightstick or similar club, and who has undergone 15 hours of training in the proper use of the club, including at least seven hours of training in the use of the club for nonviolent restraint. For the purposes of this subsection, "nonviolent restraint" means the use of reasonable force, not intended and not likely to inflict bodily injury.

(d) The provisions of Section 46.02 prohibiting the carrying of a firearm or carrying of a club do not apply to a public security officer employed by the adjutant general under Section 431.029, Government Code, in performance of official duties or while traveling to or from a place of duty.

(e) The provisions of Section 46.02 prohibiting the carrying of an illegal knife do not apply to an individual carrying a bowie knife or a sword used in a historical demonstration or in a ceremony in which the knife or sword is significant to the performance of the ceremony.

(f) Section 46.03(a)(6) does not apply to a person who possesses a firearm or club while in the actual discharge of official duties as:

(1) a member of the armed forces or state military forces, as defined by Section 431.001, Government Code; or

(2) an employee of a penal institution.

(g) The provisions of Sections 46.02 and 46.03 prohibiting the possession or carrying of a club do not apply to an animal control officer who holds a certificate issued under Section 829.006, Health and Safety Code, and who possesses or carries an instrument used specifically for deterring the bite of an animal while the officer is in the performance of official duties under the Health and Safety Code or is traveling to or from a place of duty.

(h) *[repealed by Acts 2007, 80th Leg., RS, HB 1815, §3.]

(i) *[repealed by Acts 2007, 80th Leg., RS, HB 1815, §3.]

(j) The provisions of Section 46.02 prohibiting the carrying of a handgun do not apply to an individual who carries a handgun as a participant in a historical reenactment performed in accordance with the rules of the Texas Alcoholic Beverage Commission.

Last amended by Acts 2013, 83rd Leg., R.S., Ch. 1302 (H.B. 3142), Sec. 13, eff. June 14, 2013.

Chapter 49. INTOXICATION AND ALCOHOLIC BEVERAGE OFFENSES

PC §49.01. DEFINITIONS. In this chapter:

(1) "Alcohol concentration" means the number of grams of alcohol per:

(A) 210 liters of breath;

(B) 100 milliliters of blood; or

(C) 67 milliliters of urine.

(2) "Intoxicated" means:

(A) not having the normal use of mental or physical faculties by reason of the introduction of alcohol, a controlled substance, a drug, a dangerous drug, a combination of two or more of those substances, or any other substance into the body; or

(B) having an alcohol concentration of 0.08 or more.

(3) "Motor vehicle" has the meaning assigned by Section 32.34(a).

(4) "Watercraft" means a vessel, one or more water skis, an aquaplane, or another device used for transporting or carrying a person on water, other than a device propelled only by the current of water.

(5) "Amusement ride" has the meaning assigned by Section 2151.002,

Occupations Code.
(6) "Mobile amusement ride" has the meaning assigned by Section 2151.002, Occupations Code.

Added by Acts 1993, 73rd Leg., ch. 900, Sec. 1.01, eff. Sept. 1, 1994. Amended by Acts 1999, 76th Leg., ch. 234, Sec. 1, eff. Sept. 1, 1999; Acts 1999, 76th Leg., ch. 1364, Sec. 8, eff. Jan. 1, 2000; Acts 2001, 77th Leg., ch. 1420, Sec. 14.707, eff. Sept. 1, 2001.

ALCOHOLIC BEVERAGE CODE

ABC §11.041. WARNING SIGN REQUIRED.

(a) Each holder of a permit who is not otherwise required to display a sign under Section 411.204, Government Code, shall display in a prominent place on the permit holder's premises a sign giving notice that is unlawful for a person to carry a weapon on the premises unless the weapon is a concealed handgun the person is licensed to carry under Subchapter H, Chapter 411, Government Code.

(b) The sign must be at least 6 inches high and 14 inches wide, must appear in contrasting colors, and shall be displayed in a conspicuous manner clearly visible to the public. The commission or administrator may require the permit holder to also display the sign in a language other than English if it can be observed or determined that a substantial portion of the expected customers speak the other language as their familiar language.

Last amended by Acts 2013, 83rd Leg., R.S., Ch. 1302 (H.B. 3142), Sec. 1, eff. June 14, 2013.

ABC §11.61. CANCELLATION OR SUSPENSION OF PERMIT.

(e) Except as provided by Subsection (f) or (i), the commission or administrator shall cancel an original or renewal permit if it is found, after notice and hearing, that the permittee knowingly allowed a person to possess a firearm in a building on the licensed premises. This subsection does not apply to a person:

(1) who holds a security officer commission issued under Chapter 1702, Occupations Code, if;

    (A) the person is engaged in the performance of the person's duties as a security officer,

    (B) the person is wearing a distinctive uniform; and

    (C) the weapon is in plain view;

(2) who is a peace officer;

(3) who is a permittee or an employee of a permittee if the person is supervising the operation of the premises; or

(4) who possesses a concealed handgun the person is licensed to carry under Subchapter H, Chapter 411, Government Code, unless the person is on the premises of a business described by Section 46.035(b)(1), Penal Code.

Last amended by Acts 2013, 83rd Leg., R.S., Ch. 1302 (H.B. 3142), Sec. 2, eff. June 14, 2013.

ABC §61.11. WARNING SIGN REQUIRED.

(a) Each holder of a license who is not otherwise required to display a sign under Section 411.204, Government Code, shall display in a prominent place on the license holder's premises a sign giving notice that it is unlawful for a person to carry a weapon on the premises unless the weapon is a concealed handgun the person is licensed to carry under Subchapter H, Chapter 411, Government Code.

(b) The sign must be at least 6 inches high and 14 inches wide, must appear in contrasting colors, and shall be displayed in a conspicuous manner clearly visible to the public. The commission or administrator may require the holder of the license to also display the sign in a language other than English if it can be observed or determined that a substantial portion of the expected customers speak the other language as their familiar language.

Last amended by Acts 2013, 83ʳᵈ Leg., R.S., Ch. 1302 (H.B. 3142), Sec. 3, eff. June 14, 2013.

ABC §61.71. GROUNDS FOR CANCELLATION OR SUSPENSION: RETAIL DEALER.

(f) Except as provided by Subsection (g) or (j), the commission or administrator shall cancel an original or renewal dealer's license on-premises or off-premises license if it is found, after notice and hearing, that the licensee knowingly allowed a person to possess a firearm in a building on the licensed premises. This subsection does not apply to a person:

(1) who holds a security officer commission issued under Chapter 1702, Occupations Code, if:

(A) the person is engaged in the performance of the person's duties as a security officer;

(B) the person is wearing a distinctive uniform; and

(C) the weapon is in plain view;

(2) who is a peace officer;

(3) who is a licensee or an employee of a licensee if the person is supervising the operation of the premises; or

(4) who possesses a concealed handgun the person is licensed to carry under Subchapter H, Chapter 411, Government Code, unless the person is on the premises of a business described by Section 46.035(b)(1), Penal Code.

Last amended by Acts 2013, 83ʳᵈ Leg., R.S., Ch. 1302 (H.B. 3142), Sec. 4, eff. June 14, 2013.

CIVIL PRACTICE AND REMEDIES CODE

CPRC § 83.001. CIVIL IMMUNITY. A defendant who uses force or deadly force that is justified under Chapter 9, Penal Code, is immune from civil liability for personal injury or death that results from the defendant's use of force or deadly force, as applicable.

Last amended by Acts 2007, 80ᵗʰ Leg., R.S., Ch. 1 (S.B. 378), Sec. 4, eff. Sept. 1, 2007.

CODE OF CRIMINAL PROCEDURE

CCP Art. 2.127. SCHOOL MARSHALS.

(a) Except as provided by Subsection (b), a school marshal may make arrests and exercise all authority given peace officers under this code, subject to written regulations adopted by the board of trustees of a school district or the governing body of an open-enrollment charter school under Section 37.0811, Education Code, and only act as necessary to prevent or abate the commission of an offense that threatens serious bodily injury or death of students, faculty, or visitors on school premises.

(b) A school marshal may not issue a traffic citation for a violation of Chapter 521, Transportation Code, or Subtitle C, Title 7, Transportation Code.

(c) A school marshal is not entitled to state benefits normally provided by the state to a peace officer.

(d) A person may not serve as a school marshal unless the person is:

(1) licensed under Section 1701.260, Occupations Code; and

(2) appointed by the board of trustees of a school district or the governing body of an open-enrollment charter school under Section 37.0811, Education Code.

Added by Acts 2013, 83rd Leg., R.S., Ch. 655 (H.B. 1009), Sec. 2, eff. June 14, 2013.

CCP Art. 17.292(I). MAGISTRATES ORDER FOR EMERGENCY PROTECTION.

(a) At a defendant's appearance before a magistrate after arrest for an offense involving family violence or an offense under Section 22.011, 22.021, or 42.072, Penal Code, the magistrate may issue an order for emergency protection on the magistrate's own motion or on the request of:

(1) the victim of the offense;

(2) the guardian of the victim;

(3) a peace officer; or

(4) the attorney representing the state.

(b) At a defendant's appearance before a magistrate after arrest for an offense involving family violence, the magistrate shall issue an order for emergency protection if the arrest is for an offense that also involves:

(1) serious bodily injury to the victim; or

(2) the use or exhibition of a deadly weapon during the commission of an assault.

(c) The magistrate in the order for emergency protection may prohibit the arrested party from:

(1) committing:

(A) family violence or an assault on the person protected under the order; or

(B) an act in furtherance of an offense under Section 42.072, Penal Code;

(2) communicating:

(A) directly with a member of the family or household or with the person protected under the order in a threatening or harassing manner; or

(B) a threat through any person to a member of the family or household or to the person protected under the order;

(3) going to or near:

(A) the residence, place of employment, or business of a member of the family or household or of the person protected under the order; or

(B) the residence, child care facility, or school where a child protected under the order resides or attends; or

(4) possessing a firearm, unless the person is a peace officer, as defined by Section 1.07, Penal Code, actively engaged in employment as a sworn, full-time paid employee of a state agency or political subdivision.

(d) The victim of the offense need not be present in court when the order for emergency protection is issued.

(e) In the order for emergency protection the magistrate shall specifically describe the prohibited locations and the minimum distances, if any, that the party must maintain, unless the magistrate determines for the safety of the person or persons protected by the order that specific descriptions of the locations should be omitted.

(f) To the extent that a condition imposed by an order for emergency protection issued under this article conflicts with an existing court order granting possession of or access to a child, the condition imposed under this article prevails for the duration of the order for emergency protection.

(f-1) To the extent that a condition imposed by an order issued under this article conflicts with a condition imposed by an order subsequently issued under Chapter 85, Subtitle B, Title 4, Family Code, or under Title 1 or Title 5, Family Code, the condition imposed by the order issued under the Family Code prevails.

(f-2) To the extent that a condition imposed by an order issued under this article conflicts with a condition imposed by an order subsequently issued under Chapter 83, Subtitle B, Title 4, Family Code, the condition imposed by the order issued under this article prevails unless the court issuing the order under Chapter 83, Family Code:

(1) is informed of the existence of the order issued under this article; and

(2) makes a finding in the order issued under Chapter 83, Family Code, that the court is superseding the order issued under this article.

(g) An order for emergency protection issued under this article must contain the following statements printed in bold-face type or in capital letters:

"A VIOLATION OF THIS ORDER BY COMMISSION OF AN ACT PROHIBITED BY THE ORDER MAY BE PUNISHABLE BY A FINE OF AS MUCH AS $4,000 OR BY CONFINEMENT IN JAIL FOR AS LONG AS ONE YEAR OR BY BOTH. AN ACT THAT RESULTS IN FAMILY VIOLENCE OR A STALKING OFFENSE MAY BE PROSECUTED AS A SEPARATE MISDEMEANOR OR FELONY OFFENSE. IF THE ACT IS PROSECUTED AS A SEPARATE FELONY OFFENSE, IT IS PUNISHABLE BY CONFINEMENT IN PRISON FOR AT LEAST TWO YEARS. THE POSSESSION OF A FIREARM BY A PERSON, OTHER THAN A PEACE OFFICER, AS DEFINED BY SECTION 1.07, PENAL CODE, ACTIVELY ENGAGED IN EMPLOYMENT AS A SWORN, FULL-TIME PAID EMPLOYEE OF A STATE AGENCY OR POLITICAL SUBDIVISION, WHO IS SUBJECT TO THIS ORDER MAY BE PROSECUTED AS A SEPARATE OFFENSE PUNISHABLE BY CONFINEMENT OR IMPRISONMENT.

"NO PERSON, INCLUDING A PERSON WHO IS PROTECTED BY THIS ORDER, MAY GIVE PERMISSION TO ANYONE TO IGNORE OR VIOLATE ANY PROVISION OF THIS ORDER. DURING THE TIME IN WHICH THIS ORDER IS VALID, EVERY PROVISION OF THIS ORDER IS IN FULL FORCE AND EFFECT UNLESS A COURT CHANGES THE ORDER."

(h) The magistrate issuing an order for emergency protection under this article shall send a copy of the order to the chief of police in the municipality where the member of the family or household or individual protected by the order resides, if the person resides in a municipality, or to the sheriff of the county where the person resides, if the person does not reside in a municipality. If the victim of the offense is not present when the order is issued, the magistrate issuing the order shall order an appropriate peace officer to make a good faith effort to notify, within 24 hours, the victim that the order has been issued by calling the victim's residence and place of employment. The clerk of the court shall send a copy of the order to the victim.

(i) If an order for emergency protection issued under this article prohibits a person from going to or near a child care facility or school, the magistrate shall send a copy of the order to the child care facility or school.

(j) An order for emergency protection issued under this article is effective on issuance, and the defendant shall be served a copy of the order in open court. An order for emergency protection issued under Subsection (a) or (b)(1) of this article remains in effect up to the 61st day but not less than 31 days after the date of issuance. An order for emergency protection issued under Subsection (b)(2) of this article remains in effect up to the 91st day but not less than 61 days after the date of issuance. After notice to each affected party and a hearing, the issuing court may modify all or part of an order issued under this article if the court finds that:

(1) the order as originally issued is unworkable;

(2) the modification will not place the victim of the offense at greater risk than did the original order; and

(3) the modification will not in any way endanger a person protected under the order.

(k) To ensure that an officer responding to a call is aware of the existence and terms of an order for emergency protection issued under this article, each municipal police department and sheriff shall establish a procedure within the department or office to provide adequate information or access to information for peace officers of the names of persons protected by an order for emergency protection issued under this article and of persons to whom the order is directed. The police department or sheriff may enter an order for emergency protection issued under this article in the department's or office's record of outstanding warrants as notice that the order has been issued and is in effect.

(l) In the order for emergency protection, the magistrate shall suspend a license to carry a concealed handgun issued under Subchapter H, Chapter 411, Government Code, that is held by the defendant.(m) In this article:

(1) "Family," "family violence," and "household" have the meanings assigned by Chapter 71, Family Code.

(2) "Firearm" has the meaning assigned by Chapter 46, Penal Code.

(n) On motion, notice, and hearing, or on agreement of the parties, an order for emergency protection issued under this article may be transferred to the court assuming jurisdiction over the criminal act giving rise to the issuance of the emergency order for protection. On transfer, the criminal court may modify all or part of an order issued under this subsection in the same manner and under the same standards as the issuing court under Subsection (j).

Last amended by Acts 2013, 83rd Leg., R.S., Ch. 255 (H.B. 570), Sec. 1, eff. June 14, 2013.

EDUCATION CODE

EDC §5.001. DEFINITIONS. In this subchapter:

(1) "Agency" means the Texas Education Agency.

(2) "Classroom teacher" means an educator who is employed by a school district and who, not less than an average of fours hours each day, teaches in an academic instructional setting or a career and technology instructional setting. The term does not include a teacher's aide or a full-time administrator.

Last amended by Acts 2007, 80th Leg., R.S., Ch. 1371 (S.B. 7), Sec. 1, eff. June 15, 2007.

EDC §22.081. DEFINITIONS. In this subchapter:

(1) "Department" means the Department of Public Safety.

(2) "National criminal history record information" means criminal history record information obtained from the department under Subchapter F, Chapter 411,

Government Code, and from the Federal Bureau of Investigation under Section 411.087, Government Code.

(3) "Private school" means a school that:

(A) offers a course of instruction for students in one or more grades from prekindergarten through grade 12; and

(B) is not operated by a governmental entity.

Last amended by Acts 2007, 80th Leg., R.S., Ch. 1372 (S.B. 9), Sec. 6, eff. June 15, 2007.

EDC §37.0811. SCHOOL MARSHALS.

(a) The board of trustees of a school district or the governing body of an open-enrollment charter school may appoint not more than one school marshal per 400 students in average daily attendance per campus.

(b) The board of trustees of a school district or the governing body of an open-enrollment charter school may select for appointment as a school marshal under this section an applicant who is an employee of the school district or open-enrollment charter school and certified as eligible for appointment under Section 1701.260, Occupations Code. The board of trustees or governing body may, but shall not be required to, reimburse the amount paid by the applicant to participate in the training program under that section.

(c) A school marshal appointed by the board of trustees of a school district or the governing body of an open-enrollment charter school may carry or possess a handgun on the physical premises of a school, but only:

(1) in the manner provided by written regulations adopted by the board of trustees or the governing body, and

(2) at a specific school as specified by the board of trustees or governing body, as applicable,

(d) Any written regulations adopted for purposes of Subsection (c) must provide that a school marshal may carry a concealed handgun as described by Subsection (c), except that if the primary duty of the school marshal involves regular, direct contact with students, the marshal may not carry a concealed handgun but may possess a handgun on the physical premises of a school in a locked and secured safe within the marshal's immediate reach when conducting the marshal's primary duty. The written regulations must also require that a handgun carried by or within access of a school marshal may be loaded only with frangible ammunition designed to disintegrate on impact for maximum safety and minimal danger to others.

(e) A school marshal may access a handgun under this section only under circumstances that would justify the use of deadly force under Section 9.32 or 9.33, Penal Code,

(f) A school district or charter school employee's status as a school marshal becomes inactive on:

(1) expiration of the employee's school marshal license under Section 1701.260, Occupations Code.

(2) suspension or revocation of the employee's license to carry a concealed handgun issued under Subchapter H, Chapter 411, Government Code;

(3) termination of the employee's employment with the district or charter school; or

(4) notice from the board of trustees of the district or the governing body of the charter school that the employee's services as a school marshal are no longer required.

(g) The identity of a school marshal appointed under this section is confidential, except as provided by Section 1701.260(j), Occupations Code, and is not subject to a request under Chapter 552, Government Code.

Added by Acts 2013, 83rd Leg., R.S., Ch. 655 (H.B. 1009), Sec. 3, eff. June 14, 2013.

EDC §61.003. DEFINITIONS. In this chapter:

(1) "Board" means the Texas Higher Education Coordinating Board.

(2) "Public junior college" means any junior college certified by the board in accordance with Section 61.063 of this chapter.

(3) "General academic teaching institution" means The University of Texas at Austin; The University of Texas at El Paso; The University of Texas of the Permian Basin; The University of Texas at Dallas; The University of Texas at San Antonio; Texas A&M University, Main University; The University of Texas at Arlington; Tarleton State University; Prairie View A&M University; Texas Maritime Academy; Texas Tech University; University of North Texas; Lamar University; Lamar State College-Orange; Lamar State College-Port Arthur; Texas A&M University-Kingsville; Texas A&M University-Corpus Christi; Texas Woman's University; Texas Southern University; Midwestern State University; University of Houston; University of Texas-Pan American; The University of Texas at Brownsville; Texas A&M University-Commerce; Sam Houston State University; Texas State University; West Texas A&M University; Stephen F. Austin State University; Sul Ross State University; Angelo State University; The University of Texas at Tyler; and any other college, university, or institution so classified as provided in this chapter or created and so classified, expressly or impliedly, by law.

(4) "Public senior college or university" means a general academic teaching institution as defined above.

(5) "Medical and dental unit" means The Texas A&M University System Health Science Center and its component institutions, agencies, and programs; the Texas Tech University Health Sciences Center; the Texas Tech University Health Sciences Center at El Paso; The University of Texas Medical Branch at Galveston; The University of Texas Southwestern Medical Center; The University of Texas Medical School at San Antonio; The University of Texas Dental Branch at Houston; The University of Texas M. D. Anderson Cancer Center; The University of Texas Graduate School of Biomedical Sciences at Houston; The University of Texas Dental School at San Antonio; The University of Texas Medical School at Houston; The University of Texas Health Science Center--South Texas and its component institutions, if established under Subchapter N, Chapter 74; the nursing institutions of The Texas A&M University System and The University of Texas System; and The University of Texas School of Public Health at Houston; and such other medical or dental schools as may be established by statute or as provided in this chapter.

(6) "Other agency of higher education" means The University of Texas System, System Administration; Texas Western University Museum; Texas A&M University System, Administrative and General Offices; Texas Agricultural Experiment Station; Texas Agricultural Extension Service; Rodent and Predatory Animal Control Service (a part of the Texas Agricultural Extension Service); Texas Engineering Experiment Station (including the Texas Transportation Institute); Texas Engineering Extension Service; Texas Forest Service; Texas Tech University Museum; Texas State University System, System Administration; Sam Houston Memorial Museum; Panhandle-Plains Historical Museum; Cotton Research Committee of Texas; Water Resources

Institute of Texas; Texas Veterinary Medical Diagnostic Laboratory; and any other unit, division, institution, or agency which shall be so designated by statute or which may be established to operate as a component part of any public senior college or university, or which may be so classified as provided in this chapter.

(7) "Public technical institute" means the Lamar Institute of Technology or the Texas State Technical College System.

(8) "Institution of higher education" means any public technical institute, public junior college, public senior college or university, medical or dental unit, public state college, or other agency of higher education as defined in this section.

(9) "Governing board" means the body charged with policy direction of any public technical institute, public junior college, public senior college or university, medical or dental unit, or other agency of higher education, including but not limited to boards of directors, boards of regents, boards of trustees, and independent school district boards insofar as they are charged with policy direction of a public junior college.

(10) "University system" means the association of one or more public senior colleges or universities, medical or dental units, or other agencies of higher education under the policy direction of a single governing board.

(11) "Degree program" means any grouping of subject matter courses which, when satisfactorily completed by a student, will entitle him to a degree from a public senior college or university or a medical or dental unit.

(12) "Certificate program" means a grouping of subject-matter courses which, when satisfactorily completed by a student, will entitle him to a certificate, associate degree from a technical institute or junior college, or documentary evidence, other than a degree, of completion of a course of study at the postsecondary level.

(13) "Recognized accrediting agency" means the Southern Association of Colleges and Schools and any other association or organization so designated by the board.

(14) "Educational and general buildings and facilities" means buildings and facilities essential to or commonly associated with teaching, research, or the preservation of knowledge, including the proportional share used for those activities in any building or facility used jointly with auxiliary enterprises. Excluded are auxiliary enterprise buildings and facilities, including but not limited to dormitories, cafeterias, student union buildings, stadiums, and alumni centers, used solely for those purposes.

(15) "Private or independent institution of higher education" includes only a private or independent college or university that is:

    (A) organized under the Texas Non-Profit Corporation Act (Article 1396-1.01 et seq., Vernon's Texas Civil Statutes);

    (B) exempt from taxation under Article VIII, Section 2, of the Texas Constitution and Section 501(c)(3) of the Internal Revenue Code of 1986 (26 U.S.C. Section 501); and

    (C) accredited by:

        (i) the Commission on Colleges of the Southern Association of Colleges and Schools;

        (ii) the Liaison Committee on Medical Education; or

        (iii) the American Bar Association.

(16) "Public state college" means Lamar State College--Orange, Lamar State College--Port Arthur, or the Lamar Institute of Technology.

Last amended by Acts 2013, 83ʳᵈ Leg., R.S., Ch. 179 (H.B. 1844), Sec. 6, eff. Sept. 1, 2013.

FAMILY CODE

FC §58.003. SEALING OF RECORDS.
(m) On request of the Department of Public Safety, a juvenile court shall reopen and allow the department to inspect the files and records of the juvenile court relating to an applicant for a license to carry a concealed handgun under Subchapter H, Chapter 411, Government Code.

Last amended by Acts 2013, 83ʳᵈ Leg., R.S., Ch. 1299 (H.B. 2862), Sec. 27, eff. Sept. 1, 2013.

FC §71.003. FAMILY.
"Family" includes individuals related by consanguinity or affinity, as determined under Sections 573.022 and 573.024, Government Code, individuals who are former spouses of each other, individuals who are the parents of the same child, without regard to marriage, and a foster child and foster parent, without regard to whether those individuals reside together.

Added by Acts 1997, 75ᵗʰ Leg., ch. 34, Sec. 1, eff. May 5, 1997. Amended by Acts 2001, 77ᵗʰ Leg., ch. 821, Sec. 2.03, eff. June 14, 2001.

FC §85.022. REQUIREMENTS OF ORDER APPLYING TO PERSON WHO COMMITTED FAMILY VIOLENCE.
(a) In a protective order, the court may order the person found to have committed family violence to perform acts specified by the court that the court determines are necessary or appropriate to prevent or reduce the likelihood of family violence and may order that person to:
(1) complete a battering intervention and prevention program accredited under Article 42.141, Code of Criminal Procedure;
(2) beginning on Sept. 1, 2008, if the referral option under Subdivision (1) is not available, complete a program or counsel with a provider that has begun the accreditation process described by Subsection (a-1); or
(3) if the referral option under Subdivision (1) or, beginning on Sept. 1, 2008, the referral option under Subdivision (2) is not available, counsel with a social worker, family service agency, physician, psychologist, licensed therapist, or licensed professional counselor who has completed family violence intervention training that the community justice assistance division of the Texas Department of Criminal Justice has approved, after consultation with the licensing authorities described by Chapters 152, 501, 502, 503, and 505, Occupations Code, and experts in the field of family violence.
(a-1) Beginning on Sept. 1, 2009, a program or provider serving as a referral option for the courts under Subsection (a)(1) or
(2) must be accredited under Section 4A, Article 42.141, Code of Criminal Procedure, as conforming to program guidelines under that article.
(b) In a protective order, the court may prohibit the person found to have committed family violence from:
(1) committing family violence;
(2) communicating:
　(A) directly with a person protected by an order or a member of the family or

household of a person protected by an order, in a threatening or harassing manner;

(B) a threat through any person to a person protected by an order or a member of the family or household of a person protected by an order; and

(C) if the court finds good cause, in any manner with a person protected by an order or a member of the family or household of a person protected by an order, except through the party's attorney or a per¬son appointed by the court;

(3) going to or near the residence or place of employment or business of a person protected by an order or a member of the family or household of a person protected by an order;

(4) going to or near the residence, child-care facility, or school a child protected under the order normally attends or in which the child normally resides; and

(5) engaging in conduct directed specifically toward a person who is a person protected by an order or a member of the family or house¬hold of a person protected by an order, including following the person, that is reasonably likely to harass, annoy, alarm, abuse, torment, or embarrass the person.

(6) possessing a firearm, unless the person is a peace officer, as defined by Section 1.07, Penal Code, actively engaged in employment as a sworn, full-time paid employee of a state agency or political subdivision.

(c) In an order under Subsection (b)(3) or (4), the court shall specifically describe each prohibited location and the minimum distances from the location, if any, that the party must maintain. This subsection does not apply to an order in which Section 85.007 applies.

(d) In a protective order, the court shall suspend a license to carry a concealed handgun issued under Subchapter H, Chapter 411, Government Code, that is held by a person found to have committed family violence.

Last amended by Acts 2013, 83ʳᵈ Leg., R.S., Ch. 543 (S.B. 555), Sec. 2, eff. Sept. 1, 2013.

HEALTH & SAFETY CODE

HSC §12.092. MEDICAL ADVISORY BOARD; BOARD MEMBERS.

(a) The commissioner shall appoint the medical advisory board members from:

(1) persons licensed to practice medicine in this state, including physicians who are board certified in internal medicine, psychiatry, neurology, physical medicine, or ophthalmology and who are jointly recommended by the Texas Department of Health and the Texas Medical Association; and

(2) persons licensed to practice optometry in this state who are jointly recommended by the department and the Texas Optometric Association.

(b) The medical advisory board shall assist the Department of Public Safety of the State of Texas in determining whether:

(1) an applicant for a driver's license or a license holder is capable of safely operating a motor vehicle; or

(2) an applicant for or holder of a license to carry a concealed handgun under the authority of Subchapter H, Chapter 411, Government Code, is capable of exercising sound judgment with respect to the proper use and storage of a handgun.

Last amended by Acts 2013, 83ʳᵈ Leg., R.S., Ch. 1084 (H.B. 3433), Sec. 16, eff. June 14, 2013.

HSC §12.095. BOARD PANELS; POWERS AND DUTIES.

(a) If the Department of Public Safety of the State of Texas requests an opinion or recommendation from the medical advisory board as to the ability of an applicant or license holder to operate a motor vehicle safely or to exercise sound judgment with respect to the proper use and storage of a handgun, the commissioner or a person designated by the commissioner shall convene a panel to consider the case or question submitted by that department.

(b) To take action as a panel, at least three members of the medical advisory board must be present.

(c) Each panel member shall prepare an individual independent written report for the Department of Public Safety of the State of Texas that states the member's opinion as to the ability of the applicant or license holder to operate a motor vehicle safely or to exercise sound judgment with respect to the proper use and storage of a handgun, as appropriate. In the report the panel member may also make recommendations relating to that department's subsequent action.

(d) In its deliberations, a panel may examine any medical record or report that contains material that may be relevant to the ability of the applicant or license holder.

(e) The panel may require the applicant or license holder to undergo a medical or other examination at the applicant's or holder's expense. A person who conducts an examination under this subsection may be compelled to testify before the panel and in any subsequent proceedings under Subchapter H, Chapter 411, Government Code, or Subchapter N, Chapter 521, Transportation Code, as applicable, concerning the person's observations and findings.

Last amended by Acts 2009, 81st Leg., R.S., Ch. 1146 (H.B. 2730), Sec. 11.22, eff. Sept. 1, 2009.

HSC §12.097. CONFIDENTIALITY REQUIREMENTS.

(a) All records, reports, and testimony relating to the medical condition of an applicant or license holder:

   (1) are for the confidential use of the medical advisory board, a panel, or the Department of Public Safety of the State of Texas;

   (2) are privileged information; and

   (3) may not be disclosed to any person or used as evidence in a trial except as provided by Subsection (b).

(b) In a subsequent proceeding under Subchapter H, Chapter 411, Government Code, or Subchapter N, Chapter 521, Transportation Code, the medical standards division may provide a copy of the report of the medical advisory board or panel and a medical record or report relating to an applicant or license holder to:

   (1) the Department of Public Safety of the State of Texas;

   (2) the applicant or license holder; and

   (3) the officer who presides at the hearing.

Last amended by Acts 2009, 81st Leg., R.S., Ch. 1146 (H.B. 2730), Sec. 11.22, eff. Sept. 1, 2009.

HUMAN RESOURCE CODE

HRC §80.001. FINGERPRINTING FOR IDENTIFICATION.

(a) A state law enforcement agency or the law enforcement agency of any political subdivision of the state shall comply with the request of a person to have a record of his fingerprints made or a record of the fingerprints of a child or ward of the person made.

(c) A law enforcement agency may charge a fee not to exceed $10 for the service provided under this section and may retain records of fingerprints made under this section.

Last amended by Amended by Acts 1995, 74th Leg., ch. 695, Sec. 1, eff. Sept. 1, 1995.

LABOR CODE

LC §52.061. RESTRICTION ON PROHIBITING EMPLOYEE ACCESS TO OR STORAGE OF FIREARM OR AMMUNITION.

Text of section effective on Jan. 1, 2016

A public or private employer may not prohibit an employee who holds a license to carry a handgun under Subchapter H, Chapter 411, Government Code, who otherwise lawfully possesses a firearm, or who lawfully possesses ammunition from transporting or storing a firearm or ammunition the employee is authorized by law to possess in a locked, privately owned motor vehicle in a parking lot, parking garage, or other parking area the employer provides for employees.

Added by Acts 2011, 82nd Leg., R.S., Ch. 1058 (S.B. 321), Sec. 1, eff. Sept. 1, 2011. Amended by:
Acts 2015, 84th Leg., R.S., Ch. 437 (H.B. 910), Sec. 30, eff. Jan. 1, 2016.

Text of section effective on Jan. 1, 2016

(a) Section 52.061 does not:

    (1) authorize a person who holds a license to carry a handgun under Subchapter H, Chapter 411, Government Code, who otherwise lawfully possesses a firearm, or who lawfully possesses ammunition to possess a firearm or ammunition on any property where the possession of a firearm or ammunition is prohibited by state or federal law; or

    (2) apply to:

        (A) a vehicle owned or leased by a public or private employer and used by an employee in the course and scope of the employee's employment, unless the employee is required to transport or store a firearm in the official discharge of the employee's duties;

        (B) a school district;

        (C) an open-enrollment charter school, as defined by Section 5.001, Education Code;

        (D) a private school, as defined by Section 22.081, Education Code;

        (E) property owned or controlled by a person, other than the employer, that is subject to a valid, unexpired oil, gas, or other mineral lease that contains a provision prohibiting the possession of firearms on the property; or

        (F) property owned or leased by a chemical manufacturer or oil and gas refiner with an air authorization under Chapter 382, Health and Safety Code, and on which the primary business conducted is the manufacture, use, storage, or transportation of hazardous, combustible, or explosive materials, except in regard to an employee who holds a license to carry a handgun under Subchapter H, Chapter 411, Government Code, and who stores a firearm or ammunition the employee is authorized by law to possess in a locked, privately owned motor vehicle in a parking lot, parking garage, or other parking area the employer provides for employees that is outside of a secured and restricted area:

    (i) that contains the physical plant;

    (ii) that is not open to the public; and

    (iii) the ingress into which is constantly monitored by security personnel.

(b) Section 52.061 does not prohibit an employer from prohibiting an employee who holds a license to carry a handgun under Subchapter H, Chapter 411, Government Code, or who otherwise lawfully possesses a firearm, from possessing a firearm the employee is otherwise authorized by law to possess on the premises of the employer's business. In this subsection, "premises" has the meaning assigned by Section 46.035(f)(3), Penal Code.

Added by Acts 2011, 82ⁿᵈ Leg., R.S., Ch. 1058 (S.B. 321), Sec. 1, eff. Sept. 1, 2011.
Amended by:
Acts 2015, 84th Leg., R.S., Ch. 437 (H.B. 910), Sec. 30, eff. January 1, 2016.

LC §52.063. IMMUNITY FROM CIVIL LIABILITY.

(a) Except in cases of gross negligence, a public or private employer, or the employer's principal, officer, director, employee, or agent, is not liable in a civil action for personal injury, death, property damage, or any other damages resulting from or arising out of an occurrence involving a firearm or ammunition that the employer is required to allow on the employer's property under this subchapter.

(b) The presence of a firearm or ammunition on an employer's property under the authority of this subchapter does not by itself constitute a failure by the employer to provide a safe workplace.

(c) For purposes of this section, a public or private employer, or the employer's principal, officer, director, employee, or agent, does not have a duty:

    (1) to patrol, inspect, or secure:

      (A) any parking lot, parking garage, or other parking area the employer provides for employees; or

      (B) any privately owned motor vehicle located in a parking lot, parking garage, or other parking area described by Paragraph (A); or

    (2) to investigate, confirm, or determine an employee's compliance with laws related to the ownership or possession of a firearm or ammunition or the transportation and storage of a firearm or ammunition.

Added by Acts 2011, 82ⁿᵈ Leg., R.S., Ch. 1058 (S.B. 321), Sec. 1, eff. Sept. 1, 2011.

LC §52.064. CONSTRUCTION OF PROVISION RELATING TO IMMUNITY FROM CIVIL LIABILITY.
Section 52.063 does not limit or alter the personal liability of:

(1) an individual who causes harm or injury by using a firearm or ammunition;

(2) an individual who aids, assists, or encourages another individual to cause harm or injury by using a firearm or ammunition; or

(3) an employee who transports or stores a firearm or ammunition on the property of the employee's employer but who fails to comply with the requirements of Section 52.061.

Added by Acts 2011, 82nd Leg., R.S., Ch. 1058 (S.B. 321), Sec. 1, eff. Sept. 1, 2011.

LOCAL GOVERNMENT CODE

LGC §229.001. FIREARMS; AIR GUNS; KNIVES; EXPLOSIVES.
(a) Notwithstanding any other law, including Section 43.002 of this code and Chapter 251, Agriculture Code, a municipality may not adopt regulations relating to:

(1) the transfer, private ownership, keeping, transportation, licensing, or registration of firearms, air guns, knives, ammunition, or firearm or air gun supplies; or

(2) the discharge of a firearm or air gun at a sport shooting range.

Text of subsection as amended by Acts 2015, 84th Leg., R.S.,
Ch. 700 (H.B. 905), Sec. 3
Text of subsection effective on Jan. 1, 2016

(b) Subsection (a) does not affect the authority a municipality has under another law to:

(1) require residents or public employees to be armed for personal or national defense, law enforcement, or another lawful purpose;

(2) regulate the discharge of firearms or air guns within the limits of the municipality, other than at a sport shooting range;

(3) regulate the use of property, the location of a business, or uses at a business under the municipality's fire code, zoning ordinance, or land-use regulations as long as the code, ordinance, or regulations are not used to circumvent the intent of Subsection (a) or Subdivision (5) of this subsection;

(4) regulate the use of firearms, air guns, or knives in the case of an insurrection, riot, or natural disaster if the municipality finds the regulations necessary to protect public health and safety;

(5) regulate the storage or transportation of explosives to protect public health and safety, except that 25 pounds or less of black powder for each private residence and 50 pounds or less of black powder for each retail dealer are not subject to regulation;

(6) regulate the carrying of a firearm or air gun by a person other than a person licensed to carry a handgun under Subchapter H, Chapter 411, Government Code, at a:

(A) public park;

(B) public meeting of a municipality, county, or other governmental body;

(C) political rally, parade, or official political meeting; or

(D) nonfirearms-related school, college, or professional athletic event;

(7) regulate the hours of operation of a sport shooting range, except that the hours of operation may not be more limited than the least limited hours of operation of any other business in the municipality other than a business permitted or licensed to sell or serve alcoholic beverages for on-premises consumption; or

(8) regulate the carrying of an air gun by a minor on:

(A) public property; or

(B) private property without consent of the property owner.

(c) The exception provided by Subsection (b)(6) does not apply if the firearm or air gun is in or is carried to or from an area designated for use in a lawful hunting, fishing, or other sporting event and the firearm or air gun is of the type commonly used in the activity.

(d) The exception provided by Subsection (b)(4) does not authorize the seizure or confiscation of any firearm, air gun, knife, or ammunition from an individual who is lawfully carrying or possessing the firearm, air gun, knife, or ammunition.

(e) In this section:

(1) "Air gun" means any gun that discharges a pellet, BB, or paintball by means of compressed air, gas propellant, or a spring.

(2) "Knife" has the meaning assigned by Section 46.01, Penal Code.

(3) "Sport shooting range" has the meaning assigned by Section 250.001.

(f) The attorney general may bring an action in the name of the state to obtain a temporary or permanent injunction against a municipality adopting a regulation in violation of this section.

Acts 1987, 70th Leg., ch. 149, Sec. 1, eff. Sept. 1, 1987. Amended by Acts 1995, 74th Leg., ch. 229, Sec. 7, eff. Sept. 1, 1995; Acts 1997, 75th Leg., ch. 165, Sec. 10.07, eff. Sept. 1, 1997. Renumbered from Sec. 215.001 by Acts 2001, 77th Leg., ch. 1420, Sec. 12.002(10), eff. Sept. 1, 2001.
Amended by:
Acts 2007, 80th Leg., R.S., Ch. 18 (S.B. 112), Sec. 5, eff. April 27, 2007.
Acts 2011, 82nd Leg., R.S., Ch. 624 (S.B. 766), Sec. 5, eff. September 1, 2011.
Acts 2013, 83rd Leg., R.S., Ch. 598 (S.B. 987), Sec. 1, eff. June 14, 2013.
Acts 2013, 83rd Leg., R.S., Ch. 1210 (S.B. 1400), Sec. 1, eff. June 14, 2013.
Acts 2015, 84th Leg., R.S., Ch. 437 (H.B. 910), Sec. 34, eff. January 1, 2016.
Acts 2015, 84th Leg., R.S., Ch. 700 (H.B. 905), Sec. 2, eff. September 1, 2015.
Acts 2015, 84th Leg., R.S., Ch. 700 (H.B. 905), Sec. 3, eff. September 1, 2015.

OCCUPATIONS CODE

OCC §1701.001. DEFINITIONS.

(1) "Commission" means the Texas Commission on Law Enforcement.

(2) "County jailer" means a person employed as a county jail guard under Section 85.005, Local Government Code.

(3) "Officer" means a peace officer or reserve law enforcement officer.

(4) "Peace officer" means a person elected, employed, or appointed as a peace officer under Article 2.12, Code of Criminal Procedure, or other law.

(5) "Public security officer" means a person employed or appointed as an armed security officer by this state or a political subdivision of this state. The term does not include a security officer employed by a private security company that contracts with this state or a political subdivision of this state to provide security services for the entity.

(6) "Reserve law enforcement officer" means a person designated as a reserve law enforcement officer under Section 85.004, or 341.012, Local Government Code, or Section 60.0775, Water Code.

(7) "Telecommunicator" means a person acknowledged by the commission and employed by or serving a law enforcement agency that performs law enforcement services on a 24-hour basis who receives, processes, and transmits public safety information and criminal justice data for the agency by using a base radio station on a public safety frequency regulated by the Federal Communications Commission or by another method of communication.

(8) "School marshal" means a person employed and appointed by the board of trustees of a school district or the governing body of an open-enrollment charter school under Article 2.127, Code of Criminal Procedure, and in accordance with

and having the rights provided by Section 37.0811, Education Code.

Last amended by Acts 2013, 83rd Leg., R.S., Ch. 655 (H.B. 1009), Sec. 6, eff. June 14, 2013.

OCC §1701.260. TRAINING FOR HOLDERS OF LICENSE TO CARRY A HANDGUN; CERTIFICATION OF ELIGIBILITY FOR APPOINTMENT AS SCHOOL MARSHAL.

Text of subsection effective on Jan. 1, 2016

(a) The commission shall establish and maintain a training program open to any employee of a school district, open-enrollment charter school, or public junior college who holds a license to carry a handgun issued under Subchapter H, Chapter 411, Government Code. The training may be conducted only by the commission staff or a provider approved by the commission.

(b) The commission shall collect from each person who participates in the training program identifying information that includes the person's name, the person's date of birth, the license number of the license issued to the person under Subchapter H, Chapter 411, Government Code, and the address of the person's place of employment.

(c) The training program shall include 80 hours of instruction designed to:

(1) emphasize strategies for preventing school shootings and for securing the safety of potential victims of school shootings;

(2) educate a trainee about legal issues relating to the duties of peace officers and the use of force or deadly force in the protection of others;

(3) introduce the trainee to effective law enforcement strategies and techniques;

(4) improve the trainee's proficiency with a handgun; and

(5) enable the trainee to respond to an emergency situation requiring deadly force, such as a situation involving an active shooter.

(d) The commission, in consultation with psychologists, shall devise and administer to each trainee a psychological examination to determine whether the trainee is psychologically fit to carry out the duties of a school marshal in an emergency shooting or situation involving an active shooter. The commission may license a person under this section only if the results of the examination indicate that the trainee is psychologically fit to carry out those duties.

(e) The commission shall charge each trainee a reasonable fee to cover the cost to the commission of conducting the program. The commission shall charge each person seeking renewal of a school marshal license a reasonable fee to cover the cost to the commission of renewing the person's license.

(f) The commission shall license a person who is eligible for appointment as a school marshal who:

(1) completes training under this section to the satisfaction of the commission staff; and

(2) is psychologically fit to carry out the duties of a school marshal as indicated by the results of the psychological examination administered under this section.

(g) A person's license under this section expires on the first birthday of the person occurring after the second anniversary of the date the commission licenses the person. A renewed school marshal license expires on the person's birth date, two years after the expiration of the previous license.

(h) A person may renew the school marshal license under this section by:
(1) successfully completing a renewal course designed and administered by the commission, which such license renewal training will not exceed 16 hours combined of classroom and simulation training;
(2) demonstrating appropriate knowledge on an examination designed and administered by the commission;
(3) demonstrating handgun proficiency to the satisfaction of the commission staff; and
(4) demonstrating psychological fitness on the examination described in Subsection (d).

Text of subsection effective on Jan. 1, 2016

(i) The commission shall revoke a person's school marshal license if the commission is notified by the Department of Public Safety that the person's license to carry a handgun issued under Subchapter H, Chapter 411, Government Code, has been suspended or revoked. A person whose school marshal license is revoked may obtain recertification by:
(1) furnishing proof to the commission that the person's handgun license has been reinstated; and
(2) completing the initial training under Subsection (c) to the satisfaction of the commission staff, paying the fee for the training, and demonstrating psychological fitness on the psychological examination described in Subsection (d).
(j) The commission shall submit the identifying information collected under Subsection (b) for each person licensed by the commission under this section to:
(1) the director of the Department of Public Safety;
(2) the person's employer, if the person is employed by a school district, open-enrollment charter school, or public junior college;
(3) the chief law enforcement officer of the local municipal law enforcement agency if the person is employed at a campus of a school district, open-enrollment charter school, or public junior college located within a municipality;
(4) the sheriff of the county if the person is employed at a campus of a school district, open-enrollment charter school, or public junior college that is not located within a municipality; and
(5) the chief administrator of any peace officer commissioned under Section 37.081 or 51.203, Education Code, if the person is employed at a school district or public junior college that has commissioned a peace officer under either section.
(k) The commission shall immediately report the expiration or revocation of a school marshal license to the persons listed in Subsection (j).
(l) All information collected or submitted under this section is confidential, except as provided by Subsection (j), and is not subject to disclosure under Chapter 552, Government Code.

Added by Acts 2013, 83rd Leg., R.S., Ch. 655 (H.B. 1009), Sec. 5, eff. June 14, 2013.
Amended by:
Acts 2015, 84th Leg., R.S., Ch. 437 (H.B. 910), Sec. 35, eff. January 1, 2016.
Acts 2015, 84th Leg., R.S., Ch. 437 (H.B. 910), Sec. 36, eff. January 1, 2016.
Acts 2015, 84th Leg., R.S., Ch. 1144 (S.B. 386), Sec. 3, eff. September 1, 2015.
Acts 2015, 84th Leg., R.S., Ch. 1176 (S.B. 996), Sec. 2, eff. June 19, 2015.

OCC §1701.301. LICENSE REQUIRED. Except as provided by Sections 1701.310, 1701.311, and 1701.405, a person may not appoint or employ a person to serve as an officer, county jailer, school marshal, public security officer, or telecommunicator unless the person holds an appropriate license issued by the commission.

Acts 1999, 76th Leg., ch. 388, Sec. 1, eff. Sept. 1, 1999.
Amended by:
Acts 2013, 83rd Leg., R.S., Ch. 655 (H.B. 1009), Sec. 7, eff. June 14, 2013.
Acts 2013, 83rd Leg., R.S., Ch. 968 (H.B. 1951), Sec. 3, eff. January 1, 2014.

OCC §1701.357. WEAPONS PROFICIENCY FOR CERTAIN RETIRED PEACE OFFICERS AND FEDERAL LAW ENFORCEMENT OFFICERS AND FOR FORMER RESERVE LAW ENFORCEMENT OFFICERS.

(a) This section applies to:

(1) a peace officer;

(2) a federal criminal investigator designated as a special investigator under Article 2.122, Code of Criminal Procedure;

(3) a qualified retired law enforcement officer who is entitled to carry a concealed firearm under 18 U.S.C. Section 926C and is not otherwise described by Subdivision (1) or (2), and

(4) a former reserve law enforcement officer who served in that capacity not less than a total of 15 years with one or more state or local law enforcement agencies.

(b) The head of a state or local law enforcement agency may allow an retired peace officer an opportunity to demonstrate weapons proficiency if the retired officer provides to the agency a sworn affidavit stating that:

(1) the officer:

(A) honorably retired after not less than a total of 15 years of service as a commissioned officer with one or more state or local law enforcement agencies; or

(B) before completing 15 years of service as a commissioned officer with one or more state or local law enforcement agencies, separated from employment with the agency or agencies and is a qualified retired law enforcement officer, as defined by 18 U.S.C. Section 926C;

(2) the officer's license as a commissioned officer was not revoked or suspended for any period during the officer's term of service as a commissioned officer; and

(3) the officer has no psychological or physical disability that would interfere with the officer's proper handling of a handgun.

(b-1) The head of a state or local law enforcement agency may allow a person who served as a reserve law enforcement officer as described by Subsection (a) (4) an opportunity to demonstrate weapons proficiency if the person provides to the agency a sworn affidavit stating that:

(1) the person served not less than a total of 15 years as a reserve law enforcement officer with one or more state or local law enforcement agencies;

(2) the person's appointment as a reserve law enforcement officer was not revoked or suspended for any period during the person's term of service: and

(3) the person has no psychological or physical disability that would interfere with the person's proper handling of a handgun.

(c) The agency shall establish written procedures for the issuance or denial of a certificate of proficiency under this section. The agency shall issue the certificate to a retired officer who satisfactorily demonstrates weapons proficiency under Subsection (b), provides proof that the officer is entitled to receive a pension or annuity for service with a state or local law enforcement agency that employed the retired officer does not offer a pension or annuity to its retired employees, and satisfies the written procedures established by the agency. The agency shall issue the certificate to a person described by Subsection (a)(4) who satisfactorily demonstrates weapons proficiency under Subsection (b-1). The agency shall maintain records of any person who holds a certificate issued under this section.

(d) A certificate issued under this section expires on the second anniversary of the date the certificate was issued. A person to whom this section applies may request an annual evaluation of weapons proficiency and issuance of a certificate of proficiency as needed to comply with applicable federal or other laws.

(j) On request of a person described by Subsection (a)(4) who holds a certificate of proficiency under this section, the head of the state or local law enforcement agency at which the person last served as a reserve law enforcement officer shall issue to the person identification that indicates the person's status. An identification under this subsection must include a photograph of the person.

Added by Acts 2013, 83ʳᵈ Leg., R.S., Ch. 1080 (H.B. 3370), Sec. 2, eff. Sept. 1, 2013.

PARKS AND WILDLIFE CODE

PWC §62.081. WEAPONS PROHIBITED. Except as provided in Section 62.082 of this code, no person may hunt with, possess, or shoot a firearm, bow, crossbow, slingshot, or any other weapon on or across the land of the Lower Colorado River Authority.

Added by Acts 1975, 64ᵗʰ Leg., p. 1405, ch. 545, Sec. 1, eff. Sept. 1, 1975.

PWC §62.082. TARGET RANGES, MANAGED HUNTS AND OTHER EXCEPTIONS; RULES.

(a) The Board of Directors of the Lower Colorado River Authority may lease river authority land to be used on a nonprofit basis for a target rifle or archery range.

(b) A member of the boy scouts or the girl scouts or other nonprofit public service group or organization may possess and shoot a firearm, bow, and crossbow for target or instructional purposes under the supervision of a qualified instructor registered with and approved by the Lower Colorado River Authority on ranges designated by the Lower Colorado River Authority.

(c) The Board of Directors of the Lower Colorado River Authority may authorize lawful hunting on Lower Colorado River Authority lands, consistent with sound biological management practices.

Text of subsection effective on Jan. 1, 2016

(d) Section 62.081 does not apply to:
   (1) an employee of the Lower Colorado River Authority;
   (2) a person authorized to hunt under Subsection (c);
   (3) a peace officer as defined by Article 2.12, Code of Criminal Procedure; or
   (4) a person who:
   (A) possesses a handgun and a license issued under Subchapter H, Chapter 411, Government Code, to carry a handgun; or
   (B) under circumstances in which the person would be justified in the use of

deadly force under Chapter 9, Penal Code, shoots a handgun the person is licensed to carry under Subchapter H, Chapter 411, Government Code.

Text of subsection effective on Jan. 1, 2016

(e) A state agency, including the department, the Department of Public Safety, and the Lower Colorado River Authority, may not adopt a rule that prohibits a person who possesses a license issued under Subchapter H, Chapter 411, Government Code, from entering or crossing the land of the Lower Colorado River Authority while:

(1) possessing a handgun; or

(2) under circumstances in which the person would be justified in the use of deadly force under Chapter 9, Penal Code, shooting a handgun.

Acts 1975, 64th Leg., p. 1405, ch. 545, Sec. 1, eff. Sept. 1, 1975. Amended by Acts 1997, 75th Leg., ch. 1256, Sec. 90, eff. Sept. 1, 1997.
Amended by:
Acts 2007, 80th Leg., R.S., Ch. 375 (S.B. 535), Sec. 1, eff. September 1, 2007.
Acts 2007, 80th Leg., R.S., Ch. 375 (S.B. 535), Sec. 2, eff. September 1, 2007.
Acts 2013, 83rd Leg., R.S., Ch. 1302 (H.B. 3142), Sec. 11, eff. June 14, 2013.
Acts 2015, 84th Leg., R.S., Ch. 437 (H.B. 910), Sec. 38, eff. January 1, 2016.

Texas Department of Public Safety
Austin, Texas

www.ingramcontent.com/pod-product-compliance
Lightning Source LLC
Chambersburg PA
CBHW081654270326
41933CB00017B/3172